COMPETITIVE TENDERNESS

Hannie Rayson

Current Theatre Series
Currency Press · Sydney
in association with
Playbox Theatre Centre, Monash University Melbourne

CURRENT THEATRE SERIES

First published in 1996 by
Currency Press Pty Ltd,
PO Box 452 Paddington
NSW 2021, Australia
in association with
Playbox Theatre Centre

National Library of Australia
Cataloguing-in-Publication data:

Rayson, Hannie 1957–
Competitive tenderness

ISBN 0 86819 460 3.

I. Playbox Theatre (Melbourne, Vic.).
II. Title. (Series: Current theatre series)

A822.3

Publication of this title was assisted by
the Commonwealth Government
through the Australia Council, its arts
funding and advisory body.

Set by Currency, Paddington.
Printed by Bridge Printery.

Contents

Competitive Tenderness was first produced by the Playbox Theatre Centre at The C.U.B. Malthouse, on 20 November 1996 with the following cast:

BRIAN	Max Gilles
DELIA	Doris Younane
TREV / KIMBLE / MICK	Francis Greenslade
PIGGY / ROCKO	Simon Palomares
MERLE / ROY	Monica Maughan
AMELIA	Merridy Eastman
KELVIN / DRAGI	Richard Piper
DAWN	Valerie Bader

Director, Aubrey Mellor
Designer, Shaun Gurton
Lighting Designer, Efterpi Soropos
Dramaturg, Hilary Glow

CHARACTERS

BRIAN GUEST, Mayor of Greater Burke
DELIA KIBBITRAWHIB, Receptionist
TREVOR GUEST, Dog Catcher
AMELIA STITCH, Word Processor/Receptionist
WOMAN, Volvo driver
PIGGY KATSOS, Parking Officer
ROY FERRETT, CEO's Assistant Manager
KEL CARMICHAEL, Senior Traffic Officer
MERLE PICKHAVER, Councillor, Greater Burke
ROCKO RICOTTO, Adviser to the Minister
THE HON KIMBLE FARKLEY MLA, Minister for Local Government
DELORES, Private Secretary to the Minister
DAWN SNOW, CEO, Greater Burke
MICK CURRY, Maintenance
CUSTOMER ONE
CUSTOMER TWO
DRAGI SMILEVSKI, Macedonian smallgoods magnate
LADE SMILEVSKI, son of DRAGI
MILE SMILEVSKI, son of DRAGI
MAN, Volvo driver
MRS GILLESPIE
MRS RANDALL
PHOTOGRAPHER
CLERK
GREEK ORTHODOX ARCHBISHOP

ACT ONE

SCENE ONE

The Lower Town Hall.
Organ music, or similar, plays a dirge. A large photo of Roly
McKinnon is suspended, adorned with a wreath arrangement.
BRIAN GUEST *sweeps into the space in his mayoral robes.*

BRIAN: Ladies and gentlemen, it is my melancholy duty to inform
you that our Chief Executive Officer, Roly McKinnon is ... um ...
well he's dead. Roly died in the early hours of Sunday morning.
[*Silence.*]
The funeral on Tuesday will be a private affair for Roly's family
and ... um ... friends. And a memorial service will be held on
Wednesday at The Lower Burke Town Hall. For any of you who
may require grief counselling, special arrangements have been
made. It is indeed a sad day for Greater Burke, but one in which
I hope we can remember the ... um ... contribution Roly
McKinnon made to this municipality. I would ask you all to be
patient with us over the next few weeks as we attempt to steer
the ship without our captain. But I assure you all attempts will be
made to hasten the task of finding a successor.
[*Lights reveal gathering of Council staff.*]
Now while we're all here, just a few quick announcements. I'd
like to see the following blokes sometime today. Kel. Kel
Carmichael. You here Kel? Right. Um, Ray from Waste
Management. Ray, good on you. Now Mick. Mick Curry from
Maintenance. Where are you Mick? Right. Mick, there's a tap in
the Staff room. Needs a new washer, mate. If you could give that
your top priority, that'd be good. Senior Management have
expressed their concern, Mick. It does seem to have been
dripping for ... um ... several months. So, sometime today ... or

tomorrow ... soon as you can any rate, have a look into it. Good on you.
I think congratulations are in order for Gwen Cuthbert. Gwen? Where are you? Well done. For those of you were there on Saturday night down at the footy club – top night – you'll know Gwen collected first prize in the raffle. So, good on you, Gwen. We were all very pleased to see one of our people up there.
Just a reminder please. Check with your team leaders on any change to schedules this week. And ... hold on! ... settle down ... there's a message here from the boys in Traffic. The laneway on the south border of the Town Hall is actually not a staff car park. It's a No-Standing area, and we'd ask you to respect that please. Thanks everyone.

SCENE TWO

Greater Burke Municipal Offices, Reception.
A RECEPTIONIST *answers the phone.*

DELIA [*phone*]: Greater Burke Municipal Offices. Delia speaking. How may I help you? Trev!
[*She is distracted by* TREVOR *sneaking through Reception guiltily carrying a computer and a trolley loaded up with office furniture.*]
Trev! Come 'ere. [*Phone*] What? Sorry. [*Lebanese*] Are you Lebanese? Yeah I speak Lebanese. [*To* TREV] Just put it here for a sec. I need to talk to you. [*Lebanese*] You want to know how you get Meals On Wheels? Look why don't you come down to the Town Hall and ask for me. My names's Delia. Delia. And I'll help you fill out the forms in English. OK. [*English*] No worries. [*Lebanese*] Bye.
TREV: All this to Neighbourhood House, right?
DELIA: Yep. Now Trev, this is just between you and me, right?
TREV: Right.
DELIA: Now you're not going to say anything are you?
TREV: No.

2

DELIA: Good. Now, the computer goes into the front room.

TREV: The one on the right?

DELIA: No. The one on the left. It's for the Unemployed Workers Union. OK. Got that?

TREV: Yeah.

[AMELIA *enters*.]

DELIA: Shit.

AMELIA: Hi Trev. What's all this?

TREV: Um. It's ... um. It's ... What is it Delia?.

DELIA: It's a requisition order from Community Services. Trev's very kindly offered to deliver it for them.

AMELIA: Oh yeah. Trev, you owe me five bucks.

TREV: How come?

AMELIA: For the flowers.

TREV: What flowers?

AMELIA: For Roly.

TREV: Oh.

DELIA: Here.

[*She hands* AMELIA *five dollars out of petty cash.*]

AMELIA: But that's petty cash.

DELIA: I know. Trev'll give it to me later. Won't you Trev.

AMELIA: Don't forget Trev.

DELIA: Now if you'll excuse us, Amelia.

[*Phone rings.*]

Shit. Greater Burke Municipal Offices. Delia speaking. Yeah. Hold the line please. Sorry that line's busy. Will you hold? OK.

TREV: But Roly's dead.

AMELIA: I know. It's a very sad time Trev.

TREV: So, how come we're giving him flowers?

DELIA [*pointedly*]: See you later, Mil.

AMELIA: Oh.

DELIA: Now Trev, the filing cabinet goes into the back room. That's for the play group, OK.

TREV: What about this stuff?

DELIA: That's for the Serbian male choir.

TREV: What room's that?

DELIA: Same as the Croatians. Not that they know. Same room, alternate Fridays.

3

TREV: Oh yeah.

DELIA: Now just give everything else to The Victims of Rape, Incest and Murder. They share with The Pink Pumpkin Players.

TREV: Who are they?

DELIA: They're the mob who are seeking to find their inner clown. [*An elderly* WOMAN *storms in to Reception. She is immaculately groomed and has a commanding presence.*]

WOMAN: I want to see someone in Parking.

DELIA: Excuse me, just for a tick. [*Phone*] Sorry to keep you waiting. Putting you through now. Have you got all that Trev?

TREV: Think so.

DELIA [*P.A. system*]: Kel Carmichael. Kel Carmichael to Reception please.

TREV: Excuse us.

[TREV *squeezes past her with his trolley.* PIGGY *saunters in.*]

PIGGY [*to* DELIA]: Kel's in the dunny.

DELIA: Can you help this lady please.

PIGGY [*to* WOMAN]: Yeah?

DELIA [*phone*]: Greater Burke Minicipal Offices. Delia speaking.

WOMAN: Are you a Traffic Officer?

PIGGY: Yeah.

WOMAN: Well I am not, repeat, not, paying this. This was on my windscreen, under false pretences. And there is no way, no way in this world that I am going to pay that fine. Do you understand that?

PIGGY: Can I've a look?

[*He examines the ticket.*]

Yeah. That's a No-Standing area.

WOMAN: Says who? Hmm? Where does it say that?

PIGGY: Right here.

WOMAN: No you dimwit. Where does it say it in the street?

PIGGY: Excuse me?

WOMAN: I said there is no sign. That's my point. So you can take that and put it right in the rubbish bin. And common courtesy would dictate that you should say, "I am very sorry Madam. I have made a mistake. And I'm sorry to have caused you this inconvenience."

PIGGY: There's no mistake, lady. You've parked illegally.

4

WOMAN: You tell me where the sign is. Come on. You come with me now and show me where that sign is. Come on.

PIGGY: Look, you've got the right of appeal OK.

WOMAN: I don't want the right of appeal. I want this cancelled.

PIGGY: Look Lady. The sign's there. I don't want to waste your time. I saw it there this morning.

WOMAN: Oh, so this is you, is it? You're responsible for this. What's your name?

PIGGY [*mumbling*]: Paul Katsos.

WOMAN: What?

PIGGY: Katsos. But it's not going to do you any good.

WOMAN: Don't count on it Katsops. A person in my position could make your detestable existence even more wretched than it is already. Because I know people like you. Not personally of course. But I know your type. You're a type. Grotesquely overweight. Low self esteem. Bad skin. I can pick it.

PIGGY: Listen, Lady –

WOMAN: I want to see your boss.

PIGGY: Yeah well –

WOMAN: Because you're not the boss are you? No, people like you never make it up there. You're just planning to go on for the rest of your life, skulking down alleyways fining innocent people. Because you're angry aren't you Katface? I can feel it. Deep down you're a very angry little boy. And of course you can't express it can you, because, [*She lowers her voice*] your type of person doesn't speak English very well, so you just go on pushing that anger down with more donuts and pies and fatty chippies and taking it out on people who you envy. Who drive beautiful cars that you wish you could afford but can't. And never will.

[DELIA *enters.*]

DELIA [*to* WOMAN]: Excuse me. That your Volvo out the front?

WOMAN: Yes. Why?

DELIA: I think someone's just scratched the whole side panel.

WOMAN: Oh lord!

[*She exits hurriedly.*]

PIGGY: Bitch.

[DELIA *examines a coin in her hand.*]

5

DELIA: Handy little things aren't they? Twenty cent pieces.
[*A voice is heard off stage.*]
ROY: Katsos!
[ROY FERRETT *enters.*]
Katsos! Where's Carmichael?
PIGGY: He's in the loo.
ROY: He was in the loo when I rang through half an hour ago. For a team co-ordinator he spends an inordinate amount of time in the toilet.
[PIGGY *shrugs.*]
Would you mind telling him I'd like a word.
[PIGGY *lumbers over and taps on a door. There is no answer.*]
PIGGY: Kel.
[*Silence*]
Kel.
KEL: Piss off.
PIGGY: Er ... The Chief Executive Officer's Assistant Manager'd like a word.
KEL: Tell him I'm up to my neck in paperwork.
[*Pause.*]
Piggy?
PIGGY: Yes Kel.
KEL: Tell him I'll ring him back.
PIGGY: He's right here Kel.
[*The toilet flushes and* KELVIN CARMICHAEL *emerges. He strides over to* ROY *with hand outstretched.*]
KEL: Roy! Sorry about that. We're so flat out in here a bloke doesn't get a chance –
[ROY *does not meet his handshake.*]
ROY: Wash your hands Kel.
KEL: Right.
ROY: The meeting was scheduled to start exactly seven minutes ago, Kelvin.
KEL: What meeting?
ROY: Your meeting with Brian.
PIGGY: We didn't hear about any meeting.
ROY: There was a memo sent this morning.
KEL: Not to this department.

ROY: At some later stage, I'd be curious to know why memos sent from my department to your department seem to go by rail via New Guinea. But for now, if you wouldn't mind. We're waiting on you.

[*He minces off.*]

SCENE THREE

Mayoral Office.
BRIAN *and* ROY *are in a meeting with* KEL.

BRIAN: Kel.
KEL: Yessir.
BRIAN: The Macedonian Church was firebombed on Saturday night.
KEL: I know.
ROY: You know?
KEL: Yeah.
ROY: That's interesting. He knows.
    [ROY *closes the door.*]
BRIAN: Kel. I think you should talk to us first, before you talk to the police.
KEL: What d'you mean?
BRIAN: Well we might be able to sort something out.
ROY: Let's face it Kel, it looks bad. It looks bad for the entire organisation.
KEL: What are you talking about?
BRIAN: Kel, there's been some talk. It seems that one of your blokes might have been involved.
KEL: Which one Sir?
BRIAN: The Greek.
KEL: Piggy? No sir. Not Piggy.
BRIAN: The police have shown me an identikit. It looks remarkably like Piggy.
ROY: Remarkably.
KEL: Oh sir, there are a lot of people out there who look like Piggy.
ROY: Name one Kelvin.

KEL: Um. What's his name? You know ... ? The Greek bloke.
BRIAN: Oh him.
KEL: Yeah. In High Street. The butcher.
ROY: Spiros?
KEL: Yeah. That's him.
ROY: Oh come off it.
BRIAN: Oh that bloke.
ROY: I mean he's nice. But not like Piggy.
BRIAN: Yeah, I can see that.
ROY: He doesn't have the same high cheek bones.
KEL: Sir, Piggy was at my house on Saturday night.
    [*Pause.*]
    He came for dinner, so he could not possibly be involved with
    firebombing the Macedonian Church.
BRIAN: This was at 4 o'clock in the morning.
KEL: Yessir.
ROY: He was at your house at 4am?
KEL: Yessir. We were watching a Katherine Hepburn movie.
ROY: Oh I love Katherine Hepburn.
KEL: "African Queen".
ROY: My all-time favourite.
KEL: And then after that we watched two Rita Hayworth movies.
BRIAN: Tell me this Kel. Would you be prepared to stand up and say
    that in Court?
KEL: Yessir.
ROY: And Kel. Tell me this.
KEL: Yes Roy?
ROY: Does Piggy really like Rita Hayworth?
KEL: Shit yeah. Big fan.
BRIAN: Roy?
ROY: Yessir?
BRIAN: Where's my computer?
ROY: Um when did you last have it Sir?
BRIAN: I used it this morning.
ROY: Um ... can't help you there Sir.
BRIAN [*intercom*]: Delia?
DELIA: Yes Brian?
BRIAN: I've lost my computer.

DELIA: Oh Brian. That's the second one you've lost.
BRIAN: No that was a fax machine.
DELIA: Go back and trace your steps. That's the best thing.
BRIAN: Delia. It was on my desk. It's always on my desk.
DELIA: I'll look into it Brian.
BRIAN: Thank you Delia. I'd appreciate it.

SCENE FOUR

Reception.

DELIA: Shit!
[*She dials* TREV'*s mobile.*]
Trev. It's Delia. Trev, where did you get the computer?
[*Pause.*]
Whose computer did you take?
Oh gawd. Not that Brian, Trev. The other Brian.
I meant Brian in Maintenance. The one who's redundant.
Trev. Get the computer and bring it back. Yeah. And Trev. Make
it snappy will you.

SCENE FIVE

Department of Traffic.

KEL: Piggy.
PIGGY: Yeah?
KEL: You were at my house on Saturday night, right.
PIGGY: Was I?
KEL: No.
PIGGY: Didn't think so.
KEL: Pig, you're in deep shit.
PIGGY: I didn't do it Kel.

KEL: I know. You've just got in with the wrong crowd. Betty and I have had a talk and we've decided to take you under our wing. We've decided to have a barbeque on Sunday afternoon and introduce you to some nice young folk. From the scouts.

[PIGGY *scowls*.]

PIGGY: Do I have to?

KEL: You could go to jail if you prefer.

PIGGY: Sounds nice Kel. I like barbecues.

KEL: Good.

PIGGY: D'you think I could fire it up?

KEL: I don't think so, Piggy.

[KEL *picks up the paper and walks off*.]

PIGGY: Kel, before you go.

KEL: I'm not going anywhere.

PIGGY: Oh. I thought you were going to the toilet.

KEL: I am.

PIGGY: Well can I have a word?

KEL: Can't it wait?

PIGGY: Not that long.

KEL: What is it then?

PIGGY: Kel, do you think I've got bad skin?

[KEL *stares at him*.]

KEL: Yeah.

PIGGY: How come you've never said anything before?

KEL: Well I never really looked, did I? Not like that.

PIGGY: Like what?

KEL: Well you know. Looked at you. At your ... you know ... face.

PIGGY: I've been having these dreams Kel.

KEL: Oh Gawd.

PIGGY: I dream that I keep getting violated. By women.

KEL [*brightening*]: Oh yeah?

PIGGY: I go to make out a ticket, right, and they come out of nowhere and tell me I'm a fat ugly pig and I've got no self esteem.

KEL: Yeah. I had that once.

PIGGY: What?

KEL: Low self esteem.

PIGGY: Gee Kel. You never told me that.

10

KEL: Yeah. Well. You know ...
PIGGY: How'd you get over it?
KEL: Dunno. Just went away.
PIGGY: I think women hate me.
    [DELIA *enters.*]
KEL: Nah. It's in the mind Pig. Don't worry about it.
    [DELIA *puts a schedule down on* PIGGY*'s desk.*]
DELIA: That's yours, you fat scum bag.
PIGGY: Thanks Delia.
    [DELIA *exits.*]
KEL: Got the hots for you, that one.
PIGGY: Really?
KEL: Ooh something shocking. Now if you'll excuse me. I've got a
    bit of a traffic problem, in the large intestine. Banked up from
    here to the North Road intersection.

SCENE SIX

The Offices of HON KIMBLE FARKLEY, MLA.
MERLE PICKHAVER *and* BRIAN *enter. They have been called in to
meet the Minister.* BRIAN *makes himself known to* ROCKO.

BRIAN: Brian Guest. Mayor of Greater Burke. I have a meeting with
    the Minister.
ROCKO: How do you do. Rocko Ricotto. I'm the the Minister's
    adviser.
    [*They shake hands.*]
BRIAN: And this is Mrs Pickhaver. One of our councillors. East
    Ward.
ROCKO: Merle.
MERLE: Rocko.
BRIAN: You know each other.
MERLE: Rocko and I have had run-ins before. But I didn't know
    you'd schmoozed your way into this job.
BRIAN: Merle's been very involved in the selection process for the
    CEO –

11

ROCKO: Yes. I'm sure she has. Never miss an opportunity eh Merle?

MERLE: I trust that you appreciate that the appointment of the CEO is actually a Council matter. And we'd be very concerned if there was any intention of interference from the Minister.

ROCKO: I'm sure that's not the case but you can certainly raise that with Mr Farkly.

MERLE: I intend to.

ROCKO: Excuse me for one moment, if you will.

[*He taps on the Minister's door and enters.*]

He's got Merle Pickhaver with him.

FARKLEY: Not that lezzo from the Traders' Association?

ROCKO: Nah. Not her. This one's a councillor. Big on all the community involvement crap. She's behind the Unemployed Youth Coalition; involved in the Save Edward Park protests.

FARKLEY: Loser, in other words.

ROCKO: Just watch your back. She's a tough bitch. Big mouth too.

FARKLEY: What about the Mayor?

ROCKO: Weak as piss.

FARKLEY: Good. Listen, I was just reading through the list of suggestions for the CEO. Who's this Dawn Snow?

ROCKO: She'd be good.

FARKLEY: Have you read her C.V.?

ROCKO: Yeah.

FARKLEY: She used to run the fucking prison system in Uganda.

ROCKO: I know. What's wrong with that?

FARKLEY: You want me to try and sell that to those nuff nuff's out there.

ROCKO: Well maybe you could forget to mention that bit. The thing to push with Dawn Snow is that she's one of the most successful business women in the country.

FARKLEY: Weight loss clinics?

ROCKO: Hundreds of them. You must have heard of them? "Thin Concepts"?

FARKLEY: Oh yeah. My wife did that.

ROCKO: Did it work?

FARKLEY: They give you these little tins. Tastes like cat food.

ROCKO: How disgusting!

FARKLEY: No she liked them. She must have. She put on two stone.

[*Pause.*]

But I like the sound of this woman. Someone who can clean up by convincing people to eat cat food.

ROCKO: Pretty impressive. But it's not just the cat food. She's got retail stores. Big property developments. She's hot this woman.

FARKLEY: So why would she want a job in local government?

ROCKO: I dunno.

[*Pause.*]

But you can bet your bottom dollar she'll be a damn side better than any of these other bleeding heart dickheads they've put forward.

FARKLEY: What was Roly McKinnon like?

ROCKO: He was a complete fucking idiot. You know one of those wet Lefties, droning on about "giving a voice to the community".

FARKLEY: Oh Jesus. You wonder when these fuckwits are going to wake up.

ROCKO: Well precisely. The thing is there isn't a single person on their list, apart from her, who's had any experience in the private sector.

FARKLEY: Well that's hopeless. I mean what do they think government is?

ROCKO: Who knows.

FARKLEY: This Snow woman? Is she a member of the Party?

ROCKO: No. But I seem to remember a very handsome donation, election before last. I think she's married to that merchant banker. Phil Snow?

FARKLEY: Really. Phil Snow. He could be very handy.

ROCKO: That did cross my mind.

FARKLEY: Not bad credentials then.

ROCKO: And she's a woman.

FARKLEY: Yeah. She's a woman. OK. Let's do it.

* * * * *

FARKLEY: Brian, how are you?

BRIAN: Good thanks.

FARKLEY: Mrs Pickhaver.

[MERLE *nods.*]

13

Thanks for coming in. I appreciate it. First of all I must pass on my condolences. We were all very shocked to hear the news about Roly. Very sad indeed.

MERLE: Yes it was.

BRIAN: Yes. He was a good man, Roly. I had a lot of time for him. Very decent sort of a bloke. Worked like a dog, of course, but always had time to have a bit of a yarn. One of those people equally at home talking to one of the cleaners as he was talking to one of our more senior people. Wasn't he Merle?

MERLE: Yeah.

BRIAN: Yeah. I had a lot of time for Roly. He'll be very sorely missed.

FARKLEY: The kind of person who's going to be very hard to replace. Clearly.

BRIAN: Oh. Irreplaceable. No question about that.

ROCKO: How would you describe his capacity as a manager, Brian?

BRIAN: Oh excellent. Excellent. You couldn't do better.

ROCKO: But we are talking about a fairly sizeable debt you've got down there.

BRIAN: Yes. Yes. But ... um, well, the budget is a fairly fluid type of thing of course, and we are ordering our priorities to look into some ... um more ... well cost cutting. Which we're confident that we can ... er look into. Yeah.

MERLE: We had a very serious setback with Federal Government cuts.

FARKLEY: Haven't we all, Mrs Pickhaver. But to get back to Rocko's initial point, I think this underlines the imperative for us to find the right person.

MERLE: Who finds the right person?

FARKLEY: Ah. The appointment of the CEO is entirely a matter for the Greater Burke Council. No question. That's your business. But I do want to toss around a few ideas.

See, Mrs Pickhaver, the main issue for me at this stage is how can I, as Minister for Local Government assist in increasing the participation of women. My government is of course totally committed, but I have to tell you it's a personal bug bear of mine. It's happening too slowly for my satisfaction. My own

14

wife is of course a feminist and very active in community affairs and we discuss this endlessly.

Why is it that top ranking, intelligent, competent women are not moving into local government? Now these are women who have consummate managerial skills and what I believe is often a superior understanding and sympathy for community values. So it's a question of what we can do to attract them into these roles. And I mean they're out there. I know them. They're often in business and looking for a new opportunity.

MERLE: We've had one application from a woman.

FARKLEY: Good.

MERLE: But I think I could safely say she's not appropriate.

BRIAN: No.

FARKLEY: Ah.

[*Pause.*]

Why is that?

BRIAN: She used to run the prison system in Uganda. I mean, can you believe it?

FARKLEY: No!

[*Pause.*]

That wouldn't be Dawn Snow. Couldn't be. Rocko?

ROCKO: It is possible, I suppose.

FARKLEY: Dawn Snow. Gee. You know who Dawn Snow is of course?

BRIAN: Oh ... well not ... Merle?

MERLE: Never heard of her.

FARKLEY: Course you have. She's the woman responsible for massively reforming the prison system in Africa. It's legendary.

ROCKO: Absolutely. God.

BRIAN: Oh yeah. That rings a bell.

FARKLEY: I mean I think there was talk at some stage about her being a contender for some human rights award. Isn't that right Rocko?

ROCKO: Not that she'd ever say anything.

FARKLEY: No. Too modest.

ROCKO: In fact I don't think that's public information.

FARKLEY: Ah. I've been indiscreet. Sorry. Perhaps you could keep that under your belt.

15

BRIAN: Oh absolutely. My lips are sealed. Merle.

MERLE: She runs weight loss clinics.

FARKLEY: Mmm. With a very clear social justice agenda I would have thought.

BRIAN: Well I s'ppose fat people are a bit disadvantaged. In this society. You know.

FARKLEY: I was thinking more along the lines of seeing a business opportunity and then using it to cream off funds for charitable purposes. That'd be more the Dawn Snow I know.

ROCKO: I'm just wondering what sort of opportunities she'd see in Greater Burke.

BRIAN: Well we do have a very large disadvantaged community.

FARKLEY: Oh well. That'd be it, then.

BRIAN: Big ethnic mix.

FARKLEY: Yes. That'd be attractive.

ROCKO: After Africa. Makes sense.

FARKLEY: Diversity management. That's what we want.

BRIAN: You don't think it needs to be someone local. Someone who understands the special nature of our community.

FARKLEY: Isn't that you?

BRIAN: Me? Oh thanks, but ... um ... I don't really want the job.

ROCKO: Brian, you're the Mayor.

BRIAN: Yes.

ROCKO: You've got a job.

FARKLEY: And that's why you got elected presumably. Because you're the one with the particular knowledge of your community.

BRIAN: Yes.

FARKLEY: But what Greater Burke needs is a woman who can run the organisation so that you and Mrs Pickhaver can best achieve your vision to lead Greater Burke into the twenty-first century. And to be frank, you couldn't do better than Dawn Snow.

SCENE SEVEN

Reception.
DELIA *is on the phone, whispering.*

DELIA: Look, don't worry about it. All we're doing is re-allocating resources right. It's like a grant. Think about it like that. A special purpose grant O.K? On account of Neighbourhood House not getting a cent from those bastards in Community Services.
[*Pause.*]
Yeah. That's right. They're looking at getting rid of another fifty people, you know. So fuck 'em. As soon as there's a new redundancy we move in and clean up the desk. Hang on.
[*A* CUSTOMER *comes to the counter.*]
Yeah?
CUSTOMER: My garbage didn't get collected this morning.
DELIA: Where abouts are you?
CUSTOMER: Burke Road.
DELIA: Lower Burke?
CUSTOMER: Upper Burke.
DELIA: Yeah. See we don't really deal with waste management in Upper Burke.
CUSTOMER: But I went to Upper Burke and they told me to come down here.
DELIA: Really? Lower Burke?
CUSTOMER: Yes.
DELIA: Well I don't know who told you that. All our garbage is handled from Outer Burke. We've re-structured, see.
CUSTOMER: What's that s'posed to mean?
DELIA: Well with garbage collection I think it means, they've discovered they can be more efficient if they can just do their run without having to stop.
[KEL *saunters up.*]
CUSTOMER: That'd be right. So I have to go out to Outer Burke?

17

DELIA: Looks like it. Want me to get someone to look into it?
CUSTOMER: Don't be ridiculous. I'll be dead before then.
    [*The* CUSTOMER *leaves.*]
DELIA [*phone*]: Sorry about that. Look I'll call you back OK.
KEL [*entering*]: Trev about?
DELIA: No. He's at a Dog Conference.
KEL: Oh yeah.
    [*Pause.*]
A dog conference.
DELIA: Well it's more your think tank actually. All the Dog
    Catchers in the district get together and um ...
KEL: Think.
DELIA: Yeah. Sort of. I guess they don't get time normally ...
KEL: No.
    [*Pause.*]
And Trev pushed for that, did he? More thinking time?
    [DELIA *giggles.*]
I heard a whisper this morning. 'Bout the new CEO.
DELIA: Really? Who?
KEL: A woman.
DELIA: Really. Hang on.
    [CUSTOMER TWO *arrives at the desk.*]
Can I help you?
CUSTOMER TWO: Yeah. I got a bit of a complaint.
DELIA: Really. A complaint? We don't get too many of those. How
    can I help you?
CUSTOMER TWO: We had a row o' trees planted, couple o' years
    ago. Up on the William's Hill.
KEL: Oh yeah. I know where that is.
CUSTOMER TWO: Freeway break, you know. Cut down on the noise.
    Tart up the street a bit.
DELIA: Oh yeah.
CUSTOMER TWO: Yeah. They're all dead. It's the wind. They
    weren't properly protected. But that would have been all right if
    they'd got a bit of a go on last summer. But they weren't
    watered.
DELIA: Mmm.

18

CUSTOMER TWO: But there's no point talkin' to your blokes out there. I tried that and nothin' happened. I need to see the boss.

DELIA: Got a biro? I'll give the number to ring. OO15 435 7324698 6573.

CUSTOMER TWO: What sort o' number's that?

DELIA: New Zealand.

CUSTOMER TWO: What?

DELIA: We sold our Parks and Gardens contract to New Zealand.

CUSTOMER TWO: You're kidding?

DELIA: Nup.

CUSTOMER TWO: That's a bloody joke.

DELIA: Well, they were much cheaper see. It's the Multi Nationals. They've got the game sewn up. 'Specially since they've moved into local government services.

CUSTOMER TWO: And I s'ppose all the revenue that could have been fed back into Greater Burke –

DELIA: Mmm. On a boat across the Tasman. Good isn't it?

CUSTOMER TWO: What a pack of idiots. What's this?

DELIA: Write to the Minister. That's the address.

CUSTOMER TWO: Farkley? Fat lot o' good that's gonna do.

DELIA: Did you vote for him?

CUSTOMER TWO: Come off it.

DELIA: Someone must have.

[CUSTOMER TWO *exits.*]

KEL: Jeez Delia. You should watch your back.

DELIA: No point complaining to me, Kel. What can I do about it?
[*Pause.*]
Anyway, what about the CEO?

KEL: That's all I know. Council voted six-three in favour, apparently.

DELIA: How did Merle vote?

KEL: Against.

DELIA: Shit.

SCENE EIGHT

Lower Town Hall

BRIAN: Ladies and gentlemen, it's a great pleasure to me personally to be able to introduce to you, our new Chief Executive Officer, Mrs Dawn Snow.

[*Doors open like a TV chat show. There is simulated applause as* DAWN *stands in the spotlight acknowledging her reception from the crowd. She is wearing a red suit cut low to expose a bountiful cleavage. She makes her way down to where* BRIAN *is standing, accompanied by rousing music. She gives* BRIAN *a star's kiss before taking her place.*]

DAWN: Hello all.

BRIAN: Dawn Snow, ladies and gentlemen. I think it's a great day for Greater Burke and I think it says a lot for the organisation, that we can attract a person of the dimensions of Mrs Snow.

Over the past two years we've fought a war on two fronts. On the Western front we've faced attack from Upper Burke and on our northern borders we've had a bloody battle with Outer Burke. Victory has been ours. The Town Hall, the seat of power has remained here in Lower Burke. And that is a testimony to each and every one of you. You have given outstanding service to your suburb, your country and the cause of freedom everywhere.

But the biggest challenge of all, ladies and gentlemen is the future. And that is yet to come.

DELIA [*surreptitiously*]: What a visionary.

[DAWN *looks around sharply to ascertain the source of the interruption.*]

BRIAN: Dawn Snow, ladies and gentlemen, comes to us here in Greater Burke, as a breath of fresh air. She is in fact an ambassador from the world of business, a concept which some of you might find ... interesting. What does a business person know about the processes of government? I can hear you asking.

MICK [*drunkenly*]: What does she know? 'Bout government? Anyway.

BRIAN: What?

MICK: Just asking. Like you said. You could hear us. Asking.

BRIAN: Oh. Right. Thank you Frank.

MICK: Mick.

BRIAN: Mick. Sorry. In answer to your question ...

MICK: Knock knock.

BRIAN: What?

MICK: Knock knock.

KEL: Not now Mick.

MICK: Not-now-Mick-who?

DELIA: Not-now-Mick, the Mayor's getting a bit pissed off.

PIGGY: Come on. Come with me. Excuse us. Sorry.

MICK: Knock Knock. Who's there? Dawn Snow. Piss off.

[PIGGY *assists him to the door, throws a paper dart and then locks the door.*]

[*Off*] Some of us have lost our fucking jobs.

BRIAN: Right. Where was I?

KEL: The world of business.

BRIAN: Yes. The world of business has a lot to teach us about streamlining operations ...

[*The door starts to rattle.*]

About cost effectiveness,

[*More rattling, followed by banging.*]

And competition, which is a reality in today's world.

[*The banging increases.* PIGGY *saunters over to the locked door.*]

PIGGY: Mick?

MICK: Yeah. Lemme in.

PIGGY: Piss off.

MICK: No I won't fucking piss off!!!

PIGGY: Go on. Piss off. Sorry Brian.

BRIAN: Mrs Snow has had many business ventures, all of them thriving concerns – from dieting to designer dog wear.

[*A paper dart comes sailing through the window onto the podium.* DAWN *smiles sweetly and slips out.*]

21

Clearly a person of imagination, flair, immense energy and expertise, emminence, er ... eloquence,

[*We hear a loud thump and crash, a strangled scream and then silence.* DAWN *discreetly slips back into her chair.*]

... um influence and may I say, elegance. Please welcome, Mrs Dawn Snow.

DAWN: Thank you. Thank you Brian. Mayor, distinguished guests, ladies and gentlemen and staff, I want to say at the outset how pleased I am to be here, working with you all, embarking on what I believe will be a very exciting journey. Now as you probably know, my management background is of course in obesity. Obesity management. And when I sold my business empire some months ago I thought, Dawn, after ten years in the business, you are not going to have to worry any more about weight control. But the funny thing is, as I've thought about Greater Burke and our quest to make this a greater city, I think there are issues here that we'd be wise to address. And like it or not, they are issues concerning organisational fat.

Now I have no intention of coming in here, throwing my weight around and sacking people willy nilly. I don't believe in that. But I do believe in eliminating certain functions by way of flushing out the system. Clearly what we don't want is an over-staffed organisation, because, contrary to what some people think, the over-staffed organisation does not get out more work than the leaner one. But my own view is staff numbers are not always the issue. Quite simply we may just need to train ourselves to say no to certain things we might fancy, but we know are not good for us.

You see, the main arteries of any organisation, and by that I mean the channels of communication, get blocked when certain people with old ideas become like fatty deposits which we allow to build up. And eventually the organisational pump ceases to push. Of course this is often a result of poor management, keeping up the same old methods, because "that's how we've always done things." But let me tell you, old, tired ideas tend to cluster and hang on like unwanted cellulite. And take it from me, once it's there it's damn near impossible to get rid of. So, in my experience when organisations run like that, you're not talking about belt tightening. You're talking stomach stapling.

Anyway I will be looking forward to meeting you all individually and talking through a personal plan for your goals and aspirations. And I look forward to the great challenge ahead. Any questions? Good. Let's get back to work then, shall we?

[*The group disperses.*]

MERLE: What d'you reckon?

DELIA: I think she's a fucking weirdo.

* * * * *

KEL: You know they were going to give her the Nobel Prize?

PIGGY: What for?

KEL: Dunno exactly. Brian told me.

PIGGY: Jesus.

KEL: But keep it to yourself. Hush hush, all right.

[*Pause.*]

I think it was for some work she did in Uganda, or somewhere.

PIGGY: Diet clinics?

KEL: Must have been.

PIGGY: You wouldn't have thought there'd be too many fat people in Uganda.

KEL: Yeah. Well. Fat people everywhere, Pig.

PIGGY: Global problem.

KEL: Yeah.

* * * * *

ROY: Oh Brian. I think she is astonishing. Honestly. Where did you find her? I'm reeling. To think, a woman like that, steering the ship. Greater Burke's just never going to be the same.

SCENE NINE

DAWN's office.

BRIAN: Oh Mrs Snow. You were magnificent. Truly magnificent.
DAWN: Oh Brian. Thank you. Thank you very much. But, Dawn, please.
BRIAN: Dawn. [*Beat.*] Dawn, you know if I wasn't a happily married man, I mean a very happily married man, I'd be in trouble.
DAWN: What do you mean Brian?
BRIAN: Oh. Nothing really. Just me being the Mayor and you being the Chief Executive Officer.
[*Pause.*]
Well there's a relationship, isn't there? A professional relationship of course. And there is a line. A line, you know. And somebody in my position, who wasn't happily married, might be in danger of ... um crossing it. And ... um, isn't it good. That's all. That I have a marriage, to Coral and you have ... um –
DAWN: A dead husband.
BRIAN: Oh dear. That's terrible.
DAWN: But I do have Kenny. My boy. And he gives me a reason to go on.
BRIAN: Oh yes. Yes. I've got two girls.
DAWN: How lovely.
BRIAN: And they give me ... um ...
DAWN: A reason?
BRIAN: Well I was thinking more along the lines of high blood pressure.
DAWN: And of course you've got your lovely wife. That must be very ... satisfying.
BRIAN: Yes. Yes it's a very satisfying ... um ... marriage.
DAWN: Brian, I was wondering. At some stage, when you've got a bit of time, I thought that you and I might get together and you could just go through a few things with me.

BRIAN: Of course.

DAWN: You know, things like the separate rate scheme, for example.

BRIAN: Oh that. Well that's pretty straightforward. What d'you want to know about that?

DAWN: Well things like "What is it?" for example.

BRIAN: What is it?

DAWN: Well I know what it is. Obviously. I mean separate rate scheme. That's very clear. But you know, just some of the finer points. The details. I thought we could get together. In the evening, or something.

[*Pause.*]

BRIAN: Absolutely.

SCENE TEN

A staff meeting is taking place.

DAWN: Now, there are several points which I'd like to address since we're all together which concern Compulsory Competitive Tendering.

[*There is a collective groan.*]

Regardless of what we may think about CCT I'm afraid it is non-negotiable as the first capital "C" indicates. Mr Katsos?

PIGGY: What? Sorry?

DAWN: What is the word?

DELIA: The "C" word.

PIGGY: The "C" word?

DAWN: Compulsory. Pay attention, please. It is *Compulsory* Competitive Tendering. And the meaning of the word "compulsory"? Anyone? It means to compel obedience. I'd like you all to make a little note of that.

[*The door opens and* TREVOR GUEST, *the Dog Ranger enters. He is wearing wet weather gear and a helmet with a face guard which he removes.*]

TREV: Sorry folks. Had a bit of trouble with a schnauzer down at the Bell Street shops.

BRIAN: Trevor. This is Dawn Snow our new CEO. Trevor Guest, Dog Ranger.

TREV: G'day Dawn. Geez those things have got teeth on 'em. Eh? Look like butter wouldn't melt, but don't you believe it. No siree.

BRIAN: Thank you Trev.

TREV: It had about a dozen people holed up in the Vietnamese take away. Couldn't get out. Little blighter was barkin' and snarlin'. [*He demonstrates making barking and snarling noises.*] Nearly took me hand off.

BRIAN: We're talking about Compulsory Competitive Tendering. Trev. CCT. Your team leader'll explain it to you later.

DELIA: Here. Do your footy tips while you're waiting.

TREV: Righteo.

DAWN: The fact is Greater Burke has been dragging its heels in this regard, thanks largely to my predecessor, whose many stirling qualities apparently didn't encompass any knowledge of financial management. Nevertheless we soldier on, don't we? So, we must meet our quota of fifty percent by the June quarter next year.

DELIA: Fifty percent of what?

DAWN: Fifty percent of our total budget, although of course the real target will be more like 70%.

DELIA: Seventy percent of all services have to be contracted out?

DAWN: No. I repeat 70% of the total budget. And that's one hundred percent of all services have to be contracted out, or rather, exposed to the process of tendering.

ROY: All our jobs?

DELIA: Except of course senior management. Their jobs are exempt.

PIGGY: That means –

KEL: – Job losses. That's what it means. And reductions to current wages and conditions which as a union representative and a firm believer in the principles of unionism, and the rights of the working classes, myself and my men, (and by that I'm including Delia and Amelia) are standing firm, carrying on the struggle, began by our forefathers the Tolpuddle Martyrs. And let me assure you we're not going to take this lying down.

BRIAN: Shut up Kel.

KEL: Sorry. It's something that had to be said.

DELIA: Good on you, Kel.

KEL: It needed saying.

PIGGY: Quite right.

TREV: You said it real well too Kel.

KEL: Thanks Trev.

TREV: No probs.

KEL: And another thing.

BRIAN: Oh god.

KEL [to DAWN]: And this is not because you're a woman.

DELIA: I'd quit now if I were you, Kel.

KEL: No. It's got to be said. I have problems with your appointment as manager of my blokes. Not because you're a woman, but because you know nothing about the job. I'm sorry. You know nothing about local government. Like traffic management, Local Laws. And buggerall about Trev's area. Ranging. Trapping, muzzling, and in some cases destroying. And I'm blowed if I can figure out why they appointed a person like yourself.

BRIAN: Kel, Kel, Kel. Let me step in here. Dawn is a Manager, Kel. She knows how to manage. It's the new thing. The new way. If Dawn knew how to direct traffic why would we need you? See, that's your job. That's what you're good at. Dawn's here to manage and lead Greater Burke into the twenty-first century.

TREV: Know how to shoot a dog, Dawn?

DAWN: With a gun to the head.

TREV: Ah yeah. She's on to it.

PIGGY: But she can't manage something she doesn't know anything about.

BRIAN: Of course she can Piggy. Management is something unto itself. It involves systems and strategies. It doesn't matter what one's managing as long as one is actually managing, if you see what I mean.

PIGGY: I think it sucks meself. I thought an insider shoulda got the job.

DELIA: Here here.

27

AMELIA: Excuse me. My name's Amelia. I work with Delia and on behalf of everybody in word processing I'd just like to say we think Mrs Snow's appointment is the best thing that's happened to Greater Burke in a very long time.

DELIA [aside]: You suck.

AMELIA: I'm not sucking Delia. I'm not.

DAWN: Thank you Amelia.

AMELIA: I'd just like to say there's been a continuum of phallic control in this organisation and for goddess feminists like myself ... and Delia, we know that the entire system of oppression has been perpetrated through terror, violence and the spray of semen.

BRIAN: Amelia, not in this office surely.

AMELIA: Everywhere, Brian. But most especially right here. Under our noses.

BRIAN: The smell of semen? [Leans across to DELIA] My wife hasn't mentioned this has she?

AMELIA: Brian, I don't want to be mean or anything but you are inherently evil.

KEL: Steady on, 'Mealy.

AMELIA: Not as a person but as an instrumentality of power. But now everything's changed because of Mrs Snow.

DELIA: How do you figure that out?

AMELIA: Because she's a woman obviously.

BRIAN: Obviously.

DELIA: So?

AMELIA: So, if Mrs Snow controls everything, right, and none of the men get any power we can live in peaceful harmony with all creation.

DELIA [staring intently at AMELIA]: This Mrs Snow?

AMELIA: Yes. This Mrs Snow. She's a woman Delia. She bleeds.

DELIA: You sure about that.

BRIAN: Amelia, Delia, please.

AMELIA: She has a vaginia.

BRIAN: Oh purlease.

AMELIA: Do you have a problem with that Brian? Do you Kel? Trev? Do you have a problem with Mrs Snow's vagina?

[The four men grunt in the negative.]

28

Good. Because it is the passage of blood from the vagina that counts here. That's what helps women transcend linear time and pass into a heightened state of shamanic awareness.

DELIA: And become better Chief Executive Officers.

AMELIA: Exactly. Better everything. It's because of our personal acquaintance with blood.

DELIA: Yes. I can see that with this Mrs Snow.

AMELIA: We're in touch with the cycle of life.

BRIAN: Er ... thank you Amelia. I'm sure Mrs Snow feels ... er ... Now if I could ask you all to speed up the process in finalising your LAWAS ...

TREV: What?

ROY: Local Area Work Agreements.

KEL: Oh yes. Just on that –

PIGGY: We had to cancel our team meeting.

AMELIA: Brian, you just cut across me.

BRIAN: Say Friday week, to lodge the documents –

AMELIA: Brian.

BRIAN: That's enough Amelia. You've had your go.

KEL: We need to reconvene.

PIGGY: Our consultant couldn't make it.

AMELIA: See. Mrs Snow. That is how people like me get silenced.

PIGGY: And not all of the team are here on Fridays.

AMELIA: And why certain people, male people, are free to go on their merry way committing horrific crimes to the planet.

DAWN [*standing*]: Thank you, Amelia. I have here a preliminary draft of the new organisational structure which I'd like you all to study. Take one and pass them on.
    [*She hands around a pile of thick 200 page documents.*]
    I think that may go some of the way to ameliorating your concerns Mr Carmichael, about my profound ignorance of municipal management. But as a Parking Officer I'm sure you'll have interesting views –

BRIAN [*to* PIGGY]: Is that footy tips? Sorry Dawn.

DAWN: Brian! Please!

BRIAN: Sorry Dawn.

DAWN: As I was saying, I'm always interested in hearing your views –

ROY: Well I have to say –

DAWN: At some later stage. So if you could study the draft and give me your feedback, Mr Carmichael, by say 2.30 this afternoon, particulary those hundred or so pages on the application of competitive neutrality. That'd be helpful. Thank you. Meeting closed. And Amelia, could I see you in my office please.

[DAWN *and* BRIAN *exit.*]

TREV: Jeez Kel. You're in sweet.

AMELIA: What's she want to see me for?

DELIA: Just a little Sisterly chat probably.

PIGGY: Before she sacks you.

KEL: Folks, I don't have a good feeling about this.

AMELIA: I feel sick.

[BRIAN *and* DAWN *exit.*]

* * * * *

[BRIAN *and* DAWN *are returning to their respective offices.*]

BRIAN: I'm sorry about Amelia. That reference to your, you know, was quite ... out of line.

DAWN: Women are very competitive Brian.

BRIAN: But she's a women's libber.

DAWN: Oh they're the worst. As I always say, What has the Women's Movement ever done for me?

* * * * *

TREV: What's all this, DDT business?

KEL: CCT. Well, it's like this, Trev. Look. These are our services, right.

[*He gathers around him implements from the table: salt and pepper shakers, biros, keys, tomato sauce bottle, etc.*]

This is Greater Burke, OK. [*The whole table*] And this is Waste Disposal, Building and Planning Services here, Parks and Gardens, Family and Youth Services, Aged and Disabled, Recreation, Library Services and so on.

TREV: Where's Dog Catching?

KEL: Oh here. You're in with us. Traffic and Local Laws. That's our department. Right?

TREV: Yeah. Got ya.

KEL: Now the way it used to be is that the Council used to run all this stuff. But because the government thinks we're hopeless slack arses, they want to get people in from the outside to run our services. They did it in the U.K. You remember Margaret Thatcher?

TREV: Um. Grey hair? Aged and Disabled Services?

DELIA: Yeah. That's her.

KEL: Shut up Delia. So what have we got here, Library Services? [*Tomato sauce.*]

TREV: No. That's Waste Disposal.

KEL: What's this?

TREV: Pepper.

KEL: Let's take Waste Management. You know, George, Gibbo, Colin, all those blokes. Instead of just doing their job –

TREV: Collecting rubbish.

KEL: Yeah. The government says that job, the whole service department is up for grabs. Right. So some business out there could say, "Yeah we reckon we could have a crack at running Waste Management. We'll put in a tender."

TREV: Do they have to know how to do it?

DELIA: No. They just have to be cheaper.

KEL: Anyway they put all the names of everyone who's tendering for the job, into a big box –

TREV: Like a raffle?

KEL: Yeah. Well it can be a bit like that. But they're supposed to choose the mob who can do it the most efficiently and –

DELIA: Cheaply.

KEL: Yeah.

TREV: So it's like a big competition.

KEL: That's right.

DELIA: Where the best person doesn't always win.

TREV: Are we gonna enter?

KEL: You bet.

TREV: Are we gonna win?

KEL: Trev! Is the Pope a Catholic?

SCENE ELEVEN

DAWN's *office.* AMELIA *enters.*

AMELIA: You wanted to see me.
DAWN: Yes. Come in Amelia. Sit down. What about a cup of tea?
AMELIA: No thanks.
DAWN: Coffee?
AMELIA: No thanks.
DAWN: Oh. OK.
    [*Pause.*]
    Amelia I wanted to have a little chat to you, as a sister.
AMELIA: Oh no.
DAWN: What's up?
AMELIA: Nothing.
DAWN: Oh.
    [*Pause.*]
    Amelia, I called you in because I wanted to tell you I was very impressed with you today and I feel that you're exactly the sort of person I want on my team.
AMELIA: What team is that?
DAWN: The Greater Burke team of course.
AMELIA: Oh that team.
DAWN: What team did you you think I meant?
AMELIA: I dunno.
DAWN: Amelia, in management discourse, we sometimes use a graph to understand the forces in society that pull people in different directions. This graph has a north-south axis and an east-west axis.
    [*She draws this on a white board.*]
    Down here in the south-west quadrant we have the type of person that we call "The Prisoner" and in my opinion that's the type of person Delia is. "The Prisoner" is someone who is totally

stuck. Switched off. The person who you get no response from. The person who is quite dead. Is that how you see Delia?

AMELIA: Um ...

DAWN: Of course you can't say. And I don't want you to say, because she's your colleague and I know that a person like you acts with integrity and loyalty. And I respect that. You see I put you up here, in the north-east sector. And this type of person we call "The Volunteer". A leader, a person who acts with confidence and clarity, has a sense of purpose, hears and listens to others and has a healthy self esteem. I want "Volunteers" on my team Amelia, and I can see you've exhibited all those qualities.

AMELIA: I think I might have that cup of tea.

DAWN: Later Amelia. I think we missed the moment. Now as you know, we have to move more aggressively toward a more competitive business-like environment. And part of the change I want to introduce is about the public face of the organisation. I'd like you to take over Reception.

AMELIA: But that's Delia's job.

DAWN: Not any more. I've got other plans for Delia. You see Delia, Amelia, the reality is, this organisation wants volunteers and my policy has always been, "take no prisoners".

[*There is a knock at the door.*]

ROY: Excuse me. Can I help Mrs Snow?

DAWN: Yes. Thanks Roy. Amelia, I'm wondering whether you could just pop out for a moment. I'd like a quick word with Roy.

AMELIA: Sure.

[AMELIA *exits, humming.*]

DAWN: Yes, now Roy what did I have to see you about? Where's my list?

ROY: Mrs Snow, I have to tell you, I agree with Amelia. I think your appointment is actually the best thing that's ever happened to Greater Burke. If I can just say that.

DAWN: Well thank you Roy. Thank you very much. Ah, here we are. [*List*] What have I got here? Policy and Economic Development paper, corporate strategy meeting, restructure recreation, collect dry cleaning. Roy Ferrett, ah! Terminate employment. Oh.

ROY: Terminate employment?

DAWN: Yes, I think that's what that says. My handwriting's dreadful.

ROY: Yes, that's what it says.

DAWN: That's an "e". Mmm. Sorry Roy. We won't be needing you any more. Sorry.

[*There is a knock at the door.* BRIAN *enters.*]

BRIAN: Excuse me Mrs Snow. Roy. Um ... Roy I wonder whether I could have a private word with Mrs Snow. Something's just come up.

DAWN: Yes. No problem Brian. I think we're finished here. Thanks Roy. Thanks for that.

[ROY *stands and begins to howl. He weeps on* BRIAN'*s shoulder.*]

BRIAN: Roy. Roy. Get a grip, mate.

ROY: She's just sacked me.

BRIAN: Sacked you?

ROY: Bitch.

BRIAN: Ah Roy. Settle down. That's uncalled for.

ROY: I hate her.

BRIAN: Roy, Mrs Snow's just doing her job. It's not easy Roy.

ROY: I've been here for thirteen years.

BRIAN: I know Roy.

ROY: I've given the best part of my life to this job.

BRIAN: I know.

ROY: I'm fifty-two, Brian. I've got a mortgage and two ageing parents to look after. Who's gonna give me a job?

[ROY *exits.*]

SCENE TWELVE

Reception.
DELIA *watches as a weeping* ROY *crosses the space.*

DELIA: Roy. Roy?

[ROY *acknowledges her, but cannot speak. He exits.*]

[*Suppressing tears*] [*Phone*] Trev? Delia. Roy Ferret's gone. Yeah. Can you do his desk on Monday? Thanks Trev.

SCENE THIRTEEN

DAWN's *office.*

DAWN: Brian I think we should talk.

BRIAN: Yes. Yes, I do too. I've been wanting to talk for some time now.

DAWN: So have I.

BRIAN: In fact I haven't been able to concentrate properly. I ... er ...

DAWN: Oh Brian.

BRIAN: I ... No. You go first.

DAWN: All right. I'll go first. Brian –

BRIAN: Oh Dawn.

DAWN: Brian, I don't know if you're aware of this –

BRIAN: – I think I am.

DAWN: There is actually a 4.8 million dollar shortfall? In the reserves?

BRIAN: What?

DAWN: Council has borrowed a substantial amount of money from reserves and then re-spent it.

BRIAN: No! I mean, I don't think so. That's not possible.

DAWN: I think it is Brian.

BRIAN: Well ... unless Roly was just taking advantage of our cash investments –

DAWN: To the tune of four point eight million dollars?

[*There is a tap on the door.* DELIA *enters.*]

DELIA: You wanted to see me Brian.

BRIAN: Oh. Um. I wonder if we could have some refreshments, please Delia.

DELIA: What?

DAWN: Pardon.

DELIA: What?

35

DAWN: "What can I get you, Mrs Snow?" I think would be the appropriate response, Delia.

DELIA: What? [*Beat.*] Oh. What can I get you Mrs Snow?

DAWN: Perhaps a receptionist who knocks and waits politely before being asked to enter.

BRIAN: Just tea thank you Delia. [*To* DAWN] Or perhaps Mrs Snow would like something stronger.

DAWN: At 11.30 on a Monday morning. I don't think so, Mr Guest. That's not the way we do business here, is it?

DELIA: I think he meant would you like two tea bags instead of one.

DAWN: Waste, Delia is something I think we should take a very stern view of, in the current climate.

BRIAN: Quite so.

DAWN: I take my tea black.

DELIA: Would you like me to save the bag?

BRIAN: I don't think that will be necessary.

DELIA: Good. No-one likes old bags round here.
    [*She exits.*]

DAWN: That girl has to go. I want to sack her.

BRIAN: Not Delia.

DAWN: Yes. Delia.

BRIAN: Why Dawn?

DAWN: Because I can. [*Beat.*] Because I can ... sense disloyalty, Brian.

BRIAN: No. Not Delia.

DAWN: Women's intuition, Brian. A woman knows when another woman is not entirely faithful. And Brian, as the chief what I need from my indians is committment with a capital "C".

BRIAN: Delia's not Indian. She's Lebanese.

DAWN: Anyway, Brian, I think there's something very important that you and I should discuss. You see, I don't think you've been entirely honest with me, Brian.

BRIAN: What do you mean Dawn?

DAWN: That little matter of the 4.8 million dollars was not made clear to me when I took this job. Now I just need to know Brian whether you were party to this information which you chose not to disclose, or whether all blame rests with that appalling idiot, Roly McKinnon.

BRIAN: Well, Roly ... um ... Roly had a few problems. With finances. Of course had I known ... the ... um full scale of the problem of the ... um problem I would have ... addressed it ... swiftly. But um everyone else, the other Councillors seemed quite happy, so I didn't ... um stick my neck out. So to speak.

DAWN: Even though you're the Mayor.

BRIAN: Yes. Yes, even though I am ... that.

[*There is a knock at the door.*]

DAWN: Come in.

[DELIA *enters.*]

BRIAN: Thank you Delia.

DELIA: Tea?

[*She offers it to* DAWN *who doesn't take it from her, but appears lost in thought.*]

DAWN: You see I had thought we could convert the 13 million dollar debt to interest-only loans to free up cash flow. But we probably have to address slashing the annual budget first. What do you think Delia?

DELIA: I think I'd like you to take the cup before I burn my hand off.

[DAWN *takes the cup.*]

DAWN: So you have no opinion on the eight hundred and sixty thousand dollars spent on the separate rate scheme.

DELIA: I thought it was a scandal.

DAWN: A scandal! How interesting. Do you know what it is?

DELIA: No. [*To* BRIAN] I just gave you one bag because of the new economy measures.

[DELIA *exits.*]

SCENE FOURTEEN

AMELIA *appears in an outfit that looks like a McDonald's uniform, with a little peaked cap.*

DELIA: What are you doing?

AMELIA: I'm sorry Delia. But it's for your own good.

DELIA: Excuse me.

37

AMELIA: She wants people in the north-east. And you're in the south-west. Sorry.

DELIA: What?

[*The phone rings.* AMELIA *leans over and answers in a slick sycophantic voice.*]

AMELIA: Good morning. You've rung Greater Burke Municipal Offices, Customer Service Centre and anything I can do to help will be a great pleasure for me personally. My name's Amelia. What can I do to help you have a nice day? Mrs Snow? I'm afraid that line's busy at the moment. Can I take a message? Kimble Farkley? How do I spell that?

[DELIA *grabs the phone from* AMELIA.]

DELIA: Mr Farkley. Dawn Snow speaking. Sorry about that. There's a new receptionist here and she's completely hopeless. You know how it is, getting good people. Just a nightmare. Now, how can I help you?

AMELIA [*shocked*]: Delia!

DELIA: Yes. Yes. I have an appointment with Mr Ricotto, well ... any minute now.

[*Lights up on* KIMBLE FARKLEY *talking on a mobile phone.*]

FARKLEY: Mrs Snow, I just wanted to congratulate you really, on the appointment. We were all very pleased.

DELIA: Well thank you Mr Farkley. Thank you very much. I just hope that I don't completely stuff up, you know.

[DELIA *mimics* DAWN's *trilling laugh.*]

FARKLEY: Oh.

DELIA: Well you know, it's been done before.

FARKLEY: Oh you mean that cretin, Roly McKinnon?

DELIA: No. No I didn't actually. You know Mr Farkley since I've been here I've realised what a truly great man, Roly McKinnon was. Quite unappreciated I think.

FARKLEY: Well that's very gracious of you, considering you'll have your work cut out for you getting that debt under control.

DELIA: Oh, no problem. I just wish I had one tenth of the humanity and vision that Roly McKinnon had. I'm just a grubby little capitalist really, with absolutely no people skills and not much ability at anything really. [*She trills.*]

[FARKLEY *is nonplussed.* AMELIA *grabs the phone off* DELIA.]

38

AMELIA: Hello.

[DELIA *grabs it back.*]

DELIA: Hello. Mr Farkley are you there? Sorry about that. Yes. As I was saying, I just may be the completely wrong person for this job. But, you know what they say, if you're prepared to take the risk, then I'm game. [*Laughter*]

AMELIA: Delia!

FARKLEY: Mrs Snow there is just one thing –

DELIA: Yes?

FARKLEY: Just a query really about "Thin Concepts"?

DELIA: "Thin Concepts"? What's that?

FARKLEY: Your business empire.

DELIA: Oh that. Oh dear. I've only been here a week but I feel as though I've been in local government all my life. Yes? What about it?

FARKLEY: It doesn't seem to be listed in the stock market. I mean I just happened to be going through the second tier listings and I would have thought –

[DAWN *enters.*]

DELIA: Yes. I have to go now. Thanks so much for your call. Bye.

AMELIA: Delia!

DAWN: Personal call, Delia?

DELIA: Yeah. Sorry. Just talking to my boyfriend.

AMELIA: Delia! She was talking to Kimble Farkley.

DELIA: Amelia! For god sake.

DAWN: Kimble Farkley?

DELIA [*to* AMELIA]: Do you know what this would mean for Kim if this got out! God Amelia. You are the last person I'll ever confide in again.

AMELIA: Mrs Snow. She just –

DAWN: Thank you Amelia. I wonder if you could just run a small errand for me.

DELIA: No. Let me. I'd be happy to do it. After all, Amelia's busy on Reception.

DAWN: No. Thank you anyway Delia. Amelia can do it. I just want a few things collected from the dry cleaners and [*Aside*] I have to say I'm a bit disappointed Amelia. Let's leave it at that. I think you know what I mean.

[AMELIA *exits.*]

DELIA: Please Mrs Snow. I beg you. I don't care what you do to me. But please don't tell anyone about me and Kimble. If anyone found out – you know.

DAWN: Tell me, Delia. Has Kimble, Mr Farkley ever said anything about –

DELIA: Oh god yes. I mean no. What am I saying? We never talk about work.

[*Pause.*]

DAWN: So he's never said anything about me?

DELIA: No. Never. But I did put in a good word for you. You know – once. Just because he was concerned about a few things.

DAWN: What sort of things?

DELIA: Oh well. He couldn't find your company listed anywhere. But that's nothing. Kimmy can never find anything.

DAWN: And is he planning to ... um investigate his concerns at all, do you know?

DELIA: I don't know. But I can ask him if you like?

DAWN: No! No. Let's just leave it at that shall we? OK Carry on.

DELIA: Excuse me? Carry on, here. Or should I um ...

DAWN: No. Carry on.

SCENE FIFTEEN

DAWN'*s office.*
DAWN *is working at her desk. The intercom buzzes.*

DAWN: Yes?

INTERCOM: Mrs Snow? Rocko Ricotto's here.

DAWN: Who?

INTERCOM: Oh Mrs Snow. I'm fairly sure he doesn't know a thing –

DAWN: What do you mean Delia?

INTERCOM: Well you know. 'Bout your bogus company.

DAWN: Delia. Delia!

[DAWN *gets into a bit of a flap, applying lipstick too generously over her mouth without the aid of a mirror. There is a knock at the door.* DELIA *enters.*]

Delia, I'll have you know there was nothing bogus – Mr Ricotto!

[ROCKO RICOTTO *follows.*]

Oh Mr Riccotto. How do you do. How very good of you to come. Thank you Delia.

ROCKO: Mrs Snow.

DAWN: Oh Dawn. Please. Call me Dawn.

[*He stares at her mouth then distracts himself.*]

ROCKO: The staff here are obviously very pleased to have you.

DAWN: Oh. Why do you say that?

ROCKO: The receptionist was very fullsome in singing your praises.

DAWN: Really.

[DAWN *realises something is wrong and fishes surreptitiously in her handbag for a mirror. She then seeks the opportunity to sneak a look and rectify matters, during the following exchange.*]

ROCKO: Dawn. The Minister has asked me to pass on his congratulations. He was very, very impressed with the appointment.

DAWN: How charming. And if I may say, what a wonderful Minister he is. Wonderful. Clearly a man of action and didn't we need that. My golly.

ROCKO: Indeed we did.

DAWN: Indeed we did.

ROCKO: Indeed.

DAWN: So. How are things going in there?

ROCKO: Where?

DAWN: In where you are.

ROCKO: Spring Street?

DAWN: Yes.

ROCKO: Good. Thanks.

DAWN: Good. So. What do I owe the pleasure of this visit, which I hope will be one of many? My door is always open and my phone ... always on the hook.

[*She trills with nervous laughter.* ROCKO *picks up a picture on the desk.*]

ROCKO: This yours?

41

DAWN: Yes he's mine. My baby. Kenny. He's three and a half.
ROCKO: Oh.
DAWN: Yes. Gorgeous isn't he? I named him after my husband.
ROCKO: The Merchant banker?
DAWN: No. No. The butcher.
ROCKO: He's a butcher?
DAWN: He was.
ROCKO: Oh. He was a butcher and now he's a merchant banker?
DAWN: No. No. Now he's dead.
ROCKO: Dead?
DAWN: Murdered.
ROCKO: Sorry?
DAWN: He was murdered.
ROCKO: My god.
DAWN: Yes. Tragic isn't it. And we've never got to the bottom of it. Now you didn't come here to talk about my private life, did you Mr Ricotto.
ROCKO: Rocko.
DAWN: Rocko.
ROCKO: The Minister has asked me to talk to you about some concerns he has about the actual tendering process here in Greater Burke.
DAWN: Really?
ROCKO: Yes. It does appear that the majority, not all, but the vast majority, in the past, and indeed before you took up the appointment –
DAWN: Yes.
ROCKO: Have actually been won by in-house bids.
DAWN: Yes.
ROCKO: And as you know we are very keen that competitive practice is actually supported by the executive officers.
DAWN: Yes. Quite. I've been terribly worried about this myself. I think they've only managed to contract out Parks and Gardens, Meals On Wheels and Maintenance. Everything else, so far, has been won by the old guard, so to speak.
ROCKO: Mmm.
DAWN: Mind you that's all about to change. In fact I won't feel my job's been done, in fact I won't rest, until we've moved most of

our services right out of here and into the private sector. I mean if you want a job done ask a busy person. That's what they say isn't it, and what they mean is of course, a business person. So I'm a hundred percent committed Rocko.

ROCKO: Not that we're saying privatise at all costs.

DAWN: Not at all. No. We're not saying that. No siree. We're saying best practice. We're saying in terms of cost and quality assurance we're going for the best.

ROCKO: That's right.

DAWN: Best tender, best people, best service. Best, best, best. Win, win, win. That's what we're doing.

ROCKO: Good.

DAWN: Good, good, good. Ha! Coffee?

ROCKO: Er. No thanks. Tell me, Mrs Snow –

DAWN: Yes.

ROCKO: What's the next cab off the rank?

DAWN: Er ... in terms of tenders?

ROCKO: Yes.

DAWN: Let me see. Er ... Traffic.

ROCKO: Right. And you've got some interesting looking bids have you, from the private sector, possibly?

DAWN: Yes. We do. We do. Not that I'm at liberty to discuss the details at this stage.

ROCKO: Course not.

DAWN: But suffice to say we have some very strong candidates. Very strong indeed.

ROCKO: Good. And you've got the Council behind you. Of course.

DAWN: Ah. Yes. Yes. One hundred percent. Very happy.

ROCKO: Mrs Pickhaver?

DAWN: Who?

ROCKO: Ah ha. Hah hah.

[*He laughs conspiratorially.* DAWN *joins in, not knowing what she's laughing at.*]

Not bad.

DAWN: Not bad at all.

[*They continue in this confusingly jocular vein.*]

Who?

[DAWN *keeps laughing.* ROCKO *stands abruptly.*]

ROCKO: Right. Well. Thank you for your time.
DAWN: Oh. Lovely. That it? Thank you for yours. Good. Thank you.
   Lovely.
ROCKO: OK then.
DAWN: OK then.
ROCKO: Well. Ciao.
DAWN: You're so very ... continental.
ROCKO: Bye.
DAWN: Bye.
   [ROCKO *exits.* DAWN *stands exhausted by the door.*]
   [*Intercom*] Delia?
AMELIA: This is Amelia. Delia's at lunch.
DAWN: Good. Amelia, who is Mrs Pickhaver?
AMELIA: Who?
   [*Pause.*]
   Oh Mrs Pickhaver. Merle. She used to be Mayor. Before Brian.
   She's a Councillor, East Ward.
DAWN: Oh.
AMELIA: She sort of runs everything round here. Yeah. She's a real
   powerhouse.
   [DAWN *takes her finger off the button, then presses it again.*]
DAWN: Oh Amelia.
AMELIA: Yes.
DAWN: When's the tender deadline for Traffic?
AMELIA: Tomorrow, 5pm.
DAWN: And how many have we received so far?
AMELIA: Hold on.
   [*Pause.*]
   Mrs Snow?
DAWN: Yes.
AMELIA: None. There's nothing in the box.
DAWN: Shit.
   [DAWN *paces her room.*]
   Traffic. Traffic. Who do I know?
   [*Pause.*]
   I just need someone who's looking for a business opportunity.
   [*Pause.*]
   Who?

SCENE SIXTEEN

Reception
AMELIA *and* MERLE. *Suddenly,* DRAGI SMILEVSKI *bursts in to the Reception area below.*

DRAGI [*to* AMELIA]: I want to speak to someone. I've had as much as I can bloody take.
[*He slams a parking infringement notice on the desk.*]
I not paying. You take me to court. And I'm gonna sue. I'm gonna sue that Greek bastard. I know it's him. This is seventy-third parking fine I had this year. An' I know who's doin' this. It's a vendetta against me and I'm gonna get that fat bastard. I gonna get him proper. You hear me.

MERLE: Settle down Dragi.

DRAGI: I not gonna settle ... Oh it's you. Can't you do something. You the Councillor here. This is wrong. This corrupt.

MERLE: Maybe you're going to have to stop parking your car illegally.

DRAGI [*shouting*]: I not parking my car illegal! I put my car in the spot an' he come by and put a No-Parking stand there. He do this every time. Because he know my car. And he don't like the Macedonian. So I think to myself I know what I do. I fool this bastard. I take my wife car. An' you know what? I put the money for two hour and I come back in maybe 30 minute. The meter it expire already and he put the ticket. He did that. He made it go expire. Because he don't like the Macedonian.
[PIGGY *appears edging backwards, carrying a very heavy desk with* TREVOR.]
That's him!

TREV: Oh oh.
[TREVOR *drops his end.* PIGGY *squawks.*]

DRAGI: Come 'ere you bastard!

[PIGGY *lurches forward, then drops the desk on his foot.* DRAGI *makes a lunge at* PIGGY's *neck pulling him down on top of himself.* TREV *scales the desk and jumps on both of them. The three men roll and brawl.* PIGGY *tries to escape but trips over* MERLE's *shopping trolley. Vegetables and fruit tumble out. As* MERLE *tries to right the trolley,* DRAGI *shoves* PIGGY *who falls backwards into the trolley; his large bum gets jammed.* PIGGY's *legs are flailing madly.* DRAGI *grabs wildly trying to disentangle himself from* TREV. DELIA *rushes out and tries to beat him off with a leg of lamb.* AMELIA *screams and rushes out.* BRIAN *comes out of his door and is thwacked on the head by a French stick wielded by* MERLE. *The trolley comes careering across the stage, towards* DAWN *who has poked her head out her door. She slams her door in time.* PIGGY *smashes into the door and falls out of the trolley. He trips over* BRIAN *and scrambles out* AMELIA's *door.* DRAGI *in pursuit, trips over* BRIAN *as well but opens the second door.* KEL *is revealed on the toilet.* TREV *grabs* DRAGI *and pulls him backward. The door swings ajar.* KEL *struggles to pull his pants up.* BRIAN *tries to slip out* DAWN's *door, but finds it locked. He slips into his own. Meanwhile* MERLE, DELIA *and* TREV *have managed to pin a snarling* DRAGI *to the ground.* PIGGY's *head appears around the door.*]

PIGGY [*to* DRAGI]: Hey you? That your Commodore out the front?

DRAGI: You know it is, you bastard!

PIGGY: Tsch tsch tsch. That's a No-Standing area. I'm gonna have to give you a big fine.

[MERLE *collars* PIGGY.]

MERLE: You're in deep shit over this.

[PIGGY *wriggles free, as does* DRAGI. PIGGY *races through* BRIAN's *door;* DRAGI *follows.* BRIAN *hides under the desk, cowering. The two men dance menacingly around the desk.* PIGGY *makes a break and rushes through the adjoining door into* DAWN's *office.* DRAGI *clambers over the desk in pursuit.* TREV *bursts in, throws a large net and manages to trap* BRIAN *who has bobbed up from under the desk.* BRIAN *and* TREV *scuffle.* PIGGY *hides in* DAWN's *stationery cupboard.* DRAGI *runs past the cupboard back into the hall knocking over the shopping trolley again which* MERLE *has just finished re-packing.* KEL *grabs* DRAGI. *They tussle and* DRAGI

46

is pushed into the toilet. MERLE *slams the door and locks him in. Meanwhile* TREV *is convinced he's trapped* DRAGI. *He's sitting on top of a struggling* BRIAN.]

MERLE: Somebody call the police.

KEL: Where's Katsos? Katsos!

DELIA: He went through there. [BRIAN's *door*]
[KEL *rushes into* BRIAN's *office.*]

TREV: Got him, boss.

KEL: Who?

TREV: The Macedonian.

KEL: That's Brian, you dipstick.

TREV: Oh geez.
[AMELIA *bursts in.*]

AMELIA: They're towing his car away.

KEL: Quick. Trev. Let's go. Katsos! Somebody find Katsos!
[*Everybody races out after* KEL. *Suddenly into the quietened space,* DAWN *enters carrying some documents. She surveys the mess with some displeasure, before approaching* AMELIA *at the desk.* AMELIA *glances at the cupboard nervously.*]

DAWN: Amelia, we've got a problem.

AMELIA: Yes, I think we might have.

DAWN: Amelia, when you think of parking officers, what do you think of?

AMELIA: Um. Thugs?
[*Suddenly two* YOUNG MEN *with wrap around sunglasses burst into the space.* (*Doubles with* KEL *and* TREV.) *They approach menacingly.*]
Can I help you?

LADE: We're lookin' for our ol' man.
[SMILEVSKI *starts up banging ferociously from inside the toilet.*]

AMELIA: Um. And who, who might that be?
[*Suddenly with one almighty shove of the shoulder,* DRAGI *breaks the door open. He tumbles out in a shower of toilet rolls that have rained down from a storage cupboard. He sits dazed and defeated at* DAWN's *feet.*]

DAWN: Dragi Smilevski!

DRAGI: Dawn Snow. What are *you* doing here?

DAWN: Oh Dragi. I'm so glad you're here. And these must be your lovely boys. My, haven't they grown up.

[*They grunt.*]

And what fine young men they are, too. Dragi, why don't you come into my office. I think I have a little proposition, that might interest you.

[BRIAN *staggers into the Reception area. He is still tied up in the net but at least he's upright. The* BOYS *jump to offensive positions, fists clenched.*]

DRAGI: Settle.

DAWN: Brian. Oh good, I'm glad you're here. This is Dragi Smilevski. Managing Director of Smilevski Smallgoods. I don't think you two have met. Brian Guest, our Mayor. And these are his boys. They're a credit to you Dragi.

DRAGI: Wait outside.

[BRIAN *sticks his hand through the net.* DRAGI *still seated on the floor raises a weary arm. They shake.*]

DAWN: Brian I thought Mr Smilevski and I might have a little talk. I'd ask you to join us but clearly you're a bit caught up.

[*She laughs merrily and ushers* DRAGI *into her office quickly.*]

SCENE SEVENTEEN

DAWN's *office*

DRAGI: If I ever lay eyes on that bastard, I'm telling you, that's it for him.

DAWN: Oh. What bastard is that Dragi? Come and sit down.

DRAGI: The Greek. The Parking Officer.

DAWN: Oh poor you. Look. You've got a cut. Let me get some cotton wool and make it better.

[DAWN *opens her cupboard sees* PIGGY, *gasps and closes the door quickly, locking it with the latch.*]

Dragi. I think Brian's office might be more comfortable. Why don't you come through.

[*She ushers him into* BRIAN'*s office and closes the door.*
MERLE *knocks on* DAWN'*s door.*]
MERLE: Mrs Snow? Excuse me? Mrs Snow?
[MERLE *pops her head around the corner. She hears a noise,*
"*Psst. Psst.*" *coming from the cupboard. She waits, listens
and hears it again. She approaches the double doored
cupboard and slides the latch. There is no-one there. As she
peers inside,* PIGGY *leaps out the other door and pushes her
in.* MERLE *is now locked in the cupboard.* PIGGY *tiptoes off.*]

SCENE EIGHTEEN

BRIAN'*s office.* DAWN *is playing a very coquettish game with* DRAGI
SMILEVSKI.

DAWN: Dragi, I don't like Piggy Katsos any more than you do, but I
think we've got more important things to think about right now.
And you never know. We might find him useful.
[*She hands him a large glass of whisky.*]
DRAGI: What da you mean?
DAWN: Dragi I remember how kind you were to me when Kenny
passed away.
DRAGI: Ah. My poor Dawn. I think of Kenny and my eyes swell
with tears. You know his butcher shop. They don't take my
smallgood any more.
DAWN: That's terrible.
DRAGI: I know. Don is good. But Smilevski is better.
DAWN: That's good. That's very good.
DRAGI: You try telling them that. Ah Dawn, business is bad. And
my boys –
DAWN: Your lovely boys.
DRAGI: Thugs.
DAWN: No.
DRAGI: I give those boys everything. Computers, cars, Scotch
College.
[*Pause.*]
I bankrupt myself on those boys. And you think they got a job.

DAWN: What about the business?
DRAGI: Ha! You think they wanta get their hands dirty.
DAWN: Dragi. I've got an idea!
[*There is a tap on the door.* BRIAN *enters.*]
BRIAN: Mr Smilevski, I really must express my great disappointment at your behaviour this morning.
DAWN: Brian!
BRIAN: I think that sort of thing is most uncalled for. My Councillors, my staff, we're shocked, quite frankly and I feel an apology is required.
DRAGI: I not apologise. I not paying seven thousand dollars.
DAWN: Fines? What fines?
DRAGI: Parking fines. Seven thousand dollars.
DAWN: Brian. Could I see you in my office for a moment.
BRIAN: This is your office Dawn.
DAWN: No. This is your office.
[*She indicates they retire to the next room.*]
Excuse us for a minute won't you Mr Smilevski.
[DAWN *ushers* BRIAN *into the adjacent room. She all but pushes him.*]
[*Aside to* DRAGI] Dragi. Remember what we say in the smallgoods business. There are many ways to skin a cat!

SCENE NINETEEN

DAWN's *office.*
BRIAN *hears a muffled "Help! Help!" coming from somewhere. He looks out the window, confused.* DAWN *bursts in and slams the door.*

DAWN: Brian! Make love to me. Now!
BRIAN: Dawn.
DAWN: Oh Brian. When you pushed the door open and stood there like that I was overwhelmed by desire. I felt this ache inside. I have to have you Brian. Quick.
BRIAN: Oh Dawn, Dawn.
DAWN: Brian. Brian.

[DAWN *pushes* BRIAN *back on the desk in her passionate fervour. The intercom buzzes.*]

DELIA: Mrs Snow?

DAWN: Yes.

DELIA: Is Brian there?

DAWN: Um.

DELIA: I just buzzed Brian and the Macedonian answered. He said Brian was in your office.

DAWN: Yes.

DELIA: Brian are you in yet?

BRIAN: What? Pardon?

DELIA: Are you in?

[*Pause.*]

Your wife's on the phone and you told me to tell her you're out.

BRIAN: Oh.

DELIA: So are you in?

BRIAN: Yes. No. Delia. Could you tell her I'll ring her back. Thank you Delia.

DAWN: Oh it's gone. Gone! All passion bled from my body.

BRIAN: Oh Dawn.

DAWN: No. It's gone. Too late. Please. Don't. Just go in there and tell the Macedonian we're happy to suspend all fines.

BRIAN: Dawn. I couldn't.

DAWN: Brian. One of this city's most emminent citizens was locked in a public toilet this morning. His car has subsequently been towed away while on official business negotiating a deal which may benefit this municipality to the tune of two million dollars. Suspend his fines Brian.

BRIAN: Right.

[BRIAN *exits into his own office.*]

DAWN: Oh my head!

[*She moves over to the cupboard.* BRIAN *re-enters.*]

BRIAN: Dawn?

DAWN: What?

BRIAN: Which one of us has to apologise?

DAWN: You do Brian.

BRIAN: Right. Thank you.

[*He exits.* DAWN *exits to the Reception. There is a knock at* DAWN's *door.* TREV *sticks his head around the corner. He enters whistling and puts a leaflet on her desk. He hears* MERLE's *cries from the cupboard. He opens the door.*]
TREV: Oh Mrs Pickhaver. We was wondering where you were.
  [*He barks.*]
MERLE: Oh thank god.
  [*He continues to bark.*]
MERLE: Stop that! Trev. Trevvv. Stop!
TREV: The Dog Obedience School's having a bit of a show. Here y'are.
  [*He hands her a notice and demonstrates a few dog tricks.*]
  We was hoping you'd be a judge in the clipping and grooming section.
MERLE: Trevor.
TREVOR: Yes.
MERLE: Somebody, this morning, locked a Councillor of Greater Burke in a stationery cupboard.
TREVOR: You're joking!
MERLE: Trevor, who am I?
TREVOR: You're Merle.
MERLE: And?
TREVOR: You're a Councillor.
MERLE: Of?
TREVOR: Greater Burke?
MERLE: And what's that Trevor?
TREVOR: A stationery cupboard.
MERLE: Mmm. And what's this Trevor?
TREVOR: A leaflet? 'Bout the dog show.
MERLE: Mm hmm.
  [MERLE *scrunches it into a little ball, opens the window and throws it out.*]
  Fetch!
  [*She storms out.*]

SCENE TWENTY

Meeting Room. DAWN *is in conference with* DRAGI.

DRAGI: You want me to put in a tender to run the Traffic Department?

DAWN: Yes.

DRAGI: Dawn, I'm truly flattered but I know nothing about parking.

DAWN: Excuse me. Do you think I know anything about dieting? Dragi. Listen to me. It's a business, like any other. You just employ people to wander around and stick little pieces of paper on other people's cars. And the more you stick the more money you make. It's very straightforward really.

DRAGI: Mmm. The more you stick – yes.

DAWN: And then they write and complain and you ignore it and you just go on sticking. What's hard about that? And then, at the end of the year you've made about one point four million dollars.

DRAGI: That's a lot of sticking.

DAWN: Now because I think you'd be awfully good at it, I'm going to give you some documents, financial details and so on, so your bid will look ... well, attractive. Not just to me Dragi, but to all the people on the selection panel. But you will need to form a little company.

DRAGI: Dragi Trafficking.

DAWN: No. No. Not that. Let's call it Traffic Supplies Limited, which is part owned by you and part owned by ... Traffic Investments Ltd.

DRAGI: Who are they?

DAWN: Well they're part owned by you and part owned by ... Parking Securities Ltd.

DRAGI: Who are they?

DAWN: They're also part owned by you and part owned by say, Violetta.

DRAGI: My wife.
DAWN: Mmm. Why not? See Dragi we just have to be a little careful that there's no perceived conflict of interest, here. You know, if it ever got out that you and I are ... well friends. You know, that our families have barbeques together on the weekend. That sort of thing. So it's important to let people know there are a lot of different companies and different people involved in your operation.
DRAGI: Yes. That's important.

SCENE TWENTY-ONE

The lunch room. MERLE *is using the photocopier.*

MERLE: I'm telling you I saw it with my own eyes.
DELIA: Oh. Disgusting. That is the most disgusting thing I have ever heard.
KEL: Oh come off it Delia. It's not that disgusting.
PIGGY: It's pretty disgusting.
DELIA: It is. I can't eat. Just thinking about it. [*She shudders.*]
       [AMELIA *comes in and sits a little away from everyone, opening her lunch quietly.*]
       [*To* AMELIA] Does he stick his tongue in?
KEL: Oh Delia.
DELIA: Well she's thick as thieves. She'd know.
AMELIA: Does who stick whose tongue in Delia?
DELIA: Brian. Does he stick his tongue in you know, Dawn.
AMELIA [*scoffing superciliously*]: Oh Delia. really. you're such a ... prisoner.
DELIA: What?
MERLE: Delia. I came down to book the Town Hall Thursday night.
       Senior Citz want to organise a public meeting.
DELIA: What for?
MERLE: Home help.
DELIA: But that's already been contracted out.

MERLE: Yeah, private cleaning mob. It's a disaster. Remember Lil Murphy?

KEL: Mick Murphy's wife?

DELIA: Yeah.

MERLE: Well, how d'you like this? She has Home Help once a week, right, on account of her arthritis.

DELIA: Yeah.

MERLE: So they came in last week and did a bit of a clean up and then left.

DELIA: What? No good?

MERLE: Oh they cleaned all right. Just failed to notice that Mrs Murphy was dead.

DELIA: What d'you mean dead?

MERLE: I mean dead. Deceased. Departed from this world. In her armchair.

DELIA: No!

MERLE: The lass reckons she thought she was asleep.

DELIA: As you would.

MERLE: Exactly. What with the banging on the door and the noise of the vaccuum cleaner, Lil just slept on.

KEL: Jesus.

MERLE: But at least they're value for money this mob.

DELIA: Sure. And we have to remember, dealing with dead persons is not part of the job description.

MERLE: Exactly. Multi-skilling only goes so far.

DELIA: Bastards.

SCENE TWENTY-TWO

DAWN's office.
KEL enters.

DAWN: Kel, I have to tell you that I'm not a hundred percent happy with how things are going with your department.

KEL: What d'you mean?

55

DAWN: Well, when I look at our revenue from Traffic, parking fines and what-have-you and I compare it with other municipalities, say the Shire of Berry, for example, which is roughly the same area, I see that we make about 50% of what they do.

KEL: But they've got Shopping Town see. Big money in that.

DAWN: Now Kel. I'm not being critical. Far from it. I just want to understand. To listen and understand. Now I know they have Shopping Town, but we've got four clearways and three shopping strips.

KEL: Yeah. But there's your problem. You go fining willy nilly in the shopping strips and you close them down. See? They're having enough problems as it is. I mean there's a bit of fair play in all of this. That's what I said to Brian. D'you want your revenue or d'you want your customer service.

DAWN: And what did Brian say?

KEL: Well he agreed with me. See your type of person in Berry, and no offence intended –

DAWN: None taken.

KEL: See your type of person there, in Traffic, is your sort of enemy of the working people.

DAWN: Mmm. The problem for us Kel, as you'll appreciate is that Traffic is a very competitive area and what we may find when we get tenders from private enterprise or indeed other councils, is that they can generate a great deal more income than we're presently enjoying.

KEL: But where's your customer service? Hmm?

DAWN: But how do you define customer service, Kel? In your particular work? Fining people?

KEL: Oh we've done extensive research on this. Training up our people. Workshops, that sort of thing. Customer relations. Your small talk, your little pleasantries, your smiling, very important.

DAWN: And then your fining.

KEL: Only when necessary, see.

DAWN: Yes well I do think we may have problems in explaining to Council that our customer relations is costing us half a million dollars. See I happen to know that one of our competitors, Kel –

KEL: Sorry?

DAWN: One of our competitors.

KEL: For traffic?

DAWN: Yes.

KEL: Um. There aren't any. You mean someone putting in a bid?

DAWN: Yes.

KEL: But there aren't any other tenderers.

DAWN: I'm afraid there is Kel. In fact we've had a very, very, very attractive proposal.

KEL: You're joking?

DAWN: I never joke. I don't have a sense of humour.

KEL: But no-one's even applied for specification documents.

DAWN: Kel. I've just postponed the deadline. And I've done that because we need to do some more work on your bid. As you'll appreciate I'm one hundred percent committed to keeping as many in-house teams as I possibly can. But when I get a tender from private enterprise which is as excellent as this one, my hands are tied.

KEL: Who is it? Who is this mob?

DAWN: Kel. Probity. I'm not at liberty. But as much as it pains me to tell you this, I don't think we've got a hope in Hades.

KEL: Oh jeesus.

DAWN: They've got a leaner team and they're prepared to work longer hours. Forget the nine day fortnight. What's more, they'll work to quotas. More fining, less smiling.

KEL: And no principles. You can bank on that.

DAWN: Kel, speaking of principles, I feel it'd be immoral of me, not to seed a little idea with you today. Just something to take away and think over. You're a good man, Kel, one of our best and you know Traffic better than anyone. If another group were to win the tender, they'd need a man like you. With your knowledge. Your experience.

KEL: You mean work for this other mob?

DAWN: Look it may not come to this Kel. I'm hoping with all my heart it doesn't. And I'll be doing everything humanly possible to ensure we win the contract. But I do feel sick at the thought of what might happen. If someone like you Kel, were to lose your job. I just feel sick.

KEL: You feel sick?!

DAWN: I couldn't sleep last night, Kel. I was so sick with worry. And then I had this thought. I thought OK. Worst case scenario. The private contractor wins.

What if Kel were to become redundant? We'd have to make a case, of course, that your position was no longer viable. Then, what if we organised a redunancy package on the Friday say. Kel could, to all intents and purposes start work on the Monday, doing exactly what he's been doing, just changing bosses. Then he'd have a job and a redundancy package. Worth about a hundred thousand dollars. But then I thought, no Dawn, don't be ridiculous. Kel's a public sector man. He'd never work for private enterprise, and he'll just tell you what you can do with your one hundred thousand. Don't even mention it.

KEL: Hang on a minute. Let me figure this out. What you're suggesting ...

DAWN: I'm not suggesting anything Kel. My hands are tied.

KEL: Well what you're proposing..

DAWN [*shaking her head*]: Uh! Uh! I'm doing no such thing.

KEL: Well the idea I had ...

DAWN: Yes.

KEL: Which I'm just testing out on you ...

DAWN: Good. Please. I'm always interested.

KEL: But I'm not agreeing to anything right?

DAWN: Course not. You're just floating an idea with me, because my door is always open.

KEL: If we were to submit a bid that was not attractive to Council, they'd be forced to choose these other turkeys, right? They'd win the contract and we'd all just move over to working for them. Doing the same job?

DAWN: Well not all of you. I don't think they'd want all of you. After all they've got their own team. But what they don't have is knowledge and experience of this area. They'd be well advised to keep someone from the inside.

KEL: What about Piggy?

DAWN: What about Piggy?

KEL: He knows the ropes north of Bell Street. You couldn't get a better officer when it comes to that neck of the woods.

DAWN: Indeed. We could put Piggy's name forward. I'm sure he could use the hundred thousand.

KEL: So a hundred thousand for Piggy, and a hundred thousand for me.

DAWN: Oh Kel, goodness me. No wonder the Union movement's in trouble.

KEL: Sorry?

DAWN: No Kel. No. We wouldn't get redundancies for two people. The Superannuation Board wouldn't buy it.

KEL: So Pig and Trev and all my other blokes. They'd be out?

DAWN: We could try and find something else Kel, but you know the situation.

KEL: I've worked with some of those boys for eight years, you know. We're mates. We've sort of got our way of doing things, which is pretty damn good.

DAWN: But not good enough Kel. That's the problem.

KEL: You're asking me to do the dirty on my blokes. That's what you're asking.

DAWN: Not at all Kel. Not at all. I'm just trying to help you, as any good manager, worth her salt would do – to sift through your options and sort out your priorities. Think about it Kel. You've got a wife and family. Two lovely girls. They might be well served by a private school education. Who knows. But you could certainly provide the sort of opportunities that'd give them such a good start in life. That's where your loyalty lies doesn't it? To your own family's future.

[*Lights fade to focus on* DAWN.]

See that's the question that each and every one of us has to face, Kel. When the crunch comes, perhaps we have to face the truth, do the right thing and look out for Number One.

END OF ACT ONE

ACT TWO

SCENE ONE

Reception.
AMELIA *is wearing a bright red suit identical to the one worn by* DAWN. *Reception has been "tastefully" refurnished. Phone rings.*

AMELIA: Greater Burke Municipal Offices. If you have a query about rates and valuations, press one. Building and Planning, press two. Health and Aged Services, press three. Our Customer Service Centre is open from 9am Mondays to Fridays. If you would care to speak to one of our operators please hold. [*She imitates a bar of recorded music which she cuts off abruptly.*] Hello. Customer Service. How may I help you?
[TREV *walks through Reception. He is wearing his dog catcher gear with a red bow tie.*]
Trev. What are you up to?
TREV: I'm thinking.
AMELIA: Really.
TREV [*as if by rote*]: I'm thinking about how I can undertake necessary techniques to identify and address opportunities to enhance my competitiveness.
AMELIA: I notice you're not wearing your jacket.
TREV: Yeah. It's in the van.
AMELIA: Mmm. Best to pop it on when you're walking through Reception.
TREV: I've had this idea Mil. What d'you reckon? We're nearly through with cat registration. Right. So after that I thought we could move into budgies. Lot of money in budgies.
[*An angry customer approaches the desk. An elderly* MAN.]
MAN: I want to see someone in Parking.

SCENE FOUR

DAWN'*s office.*
DAWN *is sitting on the floor amidst rheems of paper. She is doing the annual budget, using a calculator. She is only half listening to* DRAGI.

DRAGI: Dawn, I have a proposition to put to you. I know you have a little problem.
DAWN: Which particular problem are you referring to Dragi?
DRAGI: The little problem of the 4.8 million dollar shortfall.
DAWN: Oh that little problem.
DRAGI: Has it gone away yet?
DAWN: No. No. It's still here. Dragi what's fifteen percent of sixty six million, nine hundred and fifty thousand?
DRAGI: Ten million, forty-two thousand and five hundred.
DAWN: Thanks. They're so tricky aren't they, percentages? They've got me stumped, I tell you.
DRAGI: Dawn, listen to me. You have to sell some assets.
DAWN: Yes thank you Dragi. That's very helpful. Except there are no assets.
DRAGI: Oh, I think there are.
DAWN: I don't think so Dragi. Do you multiply by a hundred or divide by a hundred?
DRAGI: You divide. Dawn, next to my factory, Smilevski Smallgoods, there is some land. Is owned by you. The Council.
DAWN: Dragi –
DRAGI: You sell this land to me and I extend my premises. I put in my new state of the art machinery. You have cash flow and you offset your shortfall. Beautiful.
DAWN: Yes. Thank you Dragi. That's where the Neighbourhood House is. We can't sell that. Off you go.
DRAGI: Dawn! Is an old house. Is run down.

65

DAWN: I know that Dragi. But you have to understand that Council would never sell that house. It's a community facility.

DRAGI: Yes but I got idea for better community facility.

DAWN: What's that Dragi?

DRAGI: Parking. Big parking.

DAWN: Yes, I can see how that would be very attractive to you –

DRAGI: Half parking, half new building.

DAWN: Yes. Thanks Dragi. Haven't you got something to do in Traffic?

[*There is a knock at the door.* BRIAN *enters.*]

Oh Brian. Just the person. Cheerio Dragi.

[DRAGI *lingers.*]

BRIAN: Cheerio Dragi.

[DRAGI *exits.*]

DAWN: Brian, you know how we spend ten million dollars on community services?

BRIAN: Yes.

DAWN: And that represents about fifteen percent of our total expenditure.

BRIAN: I think so. I get a bit stumped to tell you the truth, when it comes to percentages.

DAWN: Oh do you Brian, goodness me. Now Brian, because Council refuses point blank to expose community services to the tendering process, we're not going to make our CCT target of fifty percent. And if we don't do that, in other words if we disobey the law, we're going to get in trouble with the headmaster.

BRIAN: Oh we don't want that.

DAWN: No we don't. And we certainly wouldn't want to get expelled would we?

BRIAN: We wouldn't even want to be spanked ... would we?

DAWN: No we wouldn't.

BRIAN: Dawn?

DAWN: Yes Brian?

BRIAN: Who's the headmaster?

DAWN: Kimble Farkley, pet.

BRIAN: Oh. I like it when you call me that.

DAWN: Do you, pet?

66

COMPETITIVE TENDERNESS

BY HANNIE RAYSON

CAST

BRIAN GUEST, Mayor of Greater Burke	**Max Gilles**
DELIA KIBBITRAWHIB, Receptionist	**Doris Younane**
TREVOR GUEST, Dog Catcher	**Francis Greenslade**
PIGGY KATSOS, Parking Officer	**Simon Palomares**
MERLE PICKHAVER, Councillor, Greater Burke	**Monica Maughan**
AMELIA STITCH, Word Processor / Receptionist	**Merridy Eastman**
KEL CARMICHAEL, Senior Traffic Officer	**Richard Piper**
ROY FERRETT, CEO's Assistant Manager	**Monica Maughan**
HON KIMBLE FARKLEY, Minister for Local Government	**Francis Greenslade**
ROCKO RICOTTO, Advisor to the Minister	**Simon Palomares**
DRAGI SMILEVSKI, Macedonian smallgoods magnate	**Richard Piper**
DAWN SNOW, CEO Greater Burke	**Valerie Bader**

All other characters played by the company

PRODUCTION

DIRECTOR	**Aubrey Mellor**
DESIGNER	**Shaun Gurton**
DRAMATURG	**Hilary Glow**
LIGHTING DESIGNER	**Efterpi Soropos**
ASSISTANT DIRECTOR	**Rebecca Headlam**
PRODUCTION MANAGER	**Andrew Barker**
TECHNICAL MANAGER	**Stuart McKenzie**
STAGE MANAGER	**Marnie McDonald**
ASSISTANT STAGE MANAGER	**Nick Ilton**
WARDROBE SUPERVISOR	**Jane Hyland**
WARDROBE ASSISTANT	**Sara Tinning**
WORKSHOP SUPERVISOR	**Colin Orchard**
SCENIC ARTIST	**Marie Orchard**
SET CONSTRUCTION	**Playbox Workshop Staff**

The Director and Playwright would like to thank: Doug McLeod, John Clarke, Magda Szubanski, Gerry Connolly, Chris Connelly, Belinda Davey and Tony Ayres for their contribution to the script. The Playwright wishes to acknowledge the assistance received in her research from many local government employees from councils across Melbourne.

The National is proud to sponsor The CUB Malthouse.

As part of the community, National Australia Bank is proud to support The CUB Malthouse, Melbourne's Contemporary Arts Centre. But our support of the community goes even further, with a range of banking products tailored to the needs of every individual and business in the area.

HANNIE RAYSON
PLAYWRIGHT

Hannie is the author of eight plays, including *Room to Move, Hotel Sorrento, Falling from Grace* and *Sloth*, as well as an episode from the ABC's *Seven Deadly Sins* TV series. Her most recent work, *Scenes from a Separation*, was co-written with Andrew Bovell and premiered at the MTC last year. Her plays have been performed across Australia and overseas. Last year *Hotel Sorrento* was staged as a performed reading in French at La Comedie Française in Paris and also Bonn, Germany. *Hotel Sorrento* was premiered by Playbox in 1990 and has had twenty-nine productions to date. Now a major film, *Hotel Sorrento* was nominated for ten AFI awards in 1995. Hannie is twice winner of an AWGIE for Best Play and the NSW Premier's Literary Award. She also won The Sidney Myer Performing Arts Award in 1995 and the inaugural *Age* Performing Arts Award for *Falling from Grace* which was produced by Playbox Theatre in 1993.

PLAYWRIGHT'S NOTE
As always, subject matter dictates form. A play about local government, by its very nature, needed to be a farce. This is not because local government is itself farcical. However over the past few years, change has been foisted upon it with such force and rapidity that it does appear to have become something of a comedy routine. To the casual punter like myself, once a citizen, now a customer, the changes in local government seem emblematic of many of the ideological shifts occurring not just locally, but globally.

Managerial discourse may soon be taught in primary school as another second language option. Competition policy has seeped into the collective consciousness, like an eleventh commandment. It is rapidly becoming a world where we worship at the altar of individualism, material capital and user pays. Notions of the Common Good are about as sexy as venereal disease. When Bob Dyer came on TV in *Pick-a-Box*, shouting "Howdy Customers", he didn't realise just how prescient he was being.

Having spent much of last year hanging out with dog catchers, parking officers, local government CEOs, councillors and kerbside recycling men, I am indebted to many people who so generously and cheerfully gave me their version of the chaos. This play is dedicated to all local government employees. Soldier on.

Hannie Rayson

AUBREY MELLOR
DIRECTOR

Aubrey Mellor is the Artistic Director of Playbox. Last year he directed Louis Nowra's *The Incorruptible*, which he took on national tour in 1996. Earlier this year he toured with David Williamson's *Sanctuary* to Kuala Lumpur, Hong Kong, Manila and Singapore and directed *Burning Time*. Renowned for his productions and translations of European classics, he has been Artistic Director of Jane Street Theatre, Nimrod Theatre and the QTC. Aubrey is a member of many Australian arts institutions including the National Playwrights' Conference, NIDA, the Academy of the Arts and the Performing Arts Board of the Australia Council.

VALERIE BADER
ACTOR

Valerie has been on the stage since the mid 1970s. During this time she spent two years in England where she appeared at the London Palladium and the New London Theatre. Australian theatre credits include *Barmaids* for Belvoir Street and Deckchair Theatre Company, *Summer of the Seventeenth Doll* and *Dinkum Assorted* for MTC, *Falsettos, King of Country, Darlinghurst Nights* and *Jonah Jones* for STC and *Steaming* at the Comedy Theatre. She co-wrote and starred in *Never Say Can't* which was produced by theatres in Perth, the Hunter Valley and Sydney. Valerie's television credits include *GP, A Country Practice* and *Come In Spinner*. Film credits include *Hoodwink* and *A Fish Tale*.

MERRIDY EASTMAN
ACTOR

Merridy is a NIDA graduate and has extensive acting experience in both theatre and television. Recent stage credits include *Kafka's Dick* (Athenaeum) and for the MTC: *Blabbermouth, The Dutch Courtesan, Gulliver's Travels, House of Blue Leaves, The Heidi Chronicles, Hay Fever, This Old Man Comes Rolling Home, A Christmas Carol* and *A Midsummer Night's Dream*. For the State Theatre of South Australia she performed in *Taking Steps, The Rover, Pravda* and *The Recruiting Officer*. Merridy's television credits include *The Man from Snowy River, The Glynn Nicholas Show, Boys from the Bush, Halifax, State Coroner* and *Playschool*. Film credits include *Gorilla Girls* and *Baby Bath Massacre*.

MAX GILLES
ACTOR

Max is well known for his series of satirical reviews including *A Night with the Right, A Night of National Reconciliation, The Gillies Report, Max Gillies Summit* and *Max Gillies Live at the Club Republic*. He was also the founding Chairman of The Australian Performing Group appearing between 1970 to 1979 in plays such as *The Hills Family Show, A Stretch of the Imagination, Scanlan, Dimboola* and *Marvellous Melbourne*. Other theatre credits include *A Chorus of Disapproval, The Department* and *Little Shop of Horrors*.

Qantas is
proud to support
Playbox Theatre
Centre of Monash
University

HILARY GLOW
DRAMATURG

Hilary has worked as dramaturg with Hannie Rayson for many years on her plays including *Falling from Grace* and *Scenes from a Separation*, co-written with Andrew Bovell. Hilary has served on the Drama Panel of the Australia Council and Arts Victoria. Currently, she manages the Women's Program at the Australian Film Commission.

FRANCIS GREENSLADE
ACTOR

Francis is well known for his regular appearances in the television comedy show *Full Frontal*. His other television credits include *Blue Heelers, Janus, Mercury* and *World Series Debating*. Theatre work includes *Macbeth* and *Blabbermouth* for MTC, *The Club* (Australian Playhouse), *The Emperor's New Clothes* (Arena), *Accidental Death of an Anarchist, Cosi, School for Scandal, Marat/Sade* and *The Tempest* for the State Theatre Company of South Australia and *Funerals & Circuses* for Magpie.

Culinary and Cultural Oasis... Healthy Homemade food in a wonderful atmosphere...

The Malthouse Café has fresh muffins, bountiful lunch rolls, tasty frittatas, pies and salads, healthy soups and tempting daily specials. And of course, we make sublime coffee and cakes (the tira mi su is truly indulgent!)

Or relax with a beer or wine in our courtyard.

We're open from 8am weekdays and from midday on weekends.

malthouse café

113 sturt street south melbourne 3205 telephone 96 85 51 05

SHAUN GURTON
DESIGNER

Shaun has worked professionally in the theatre since 1970 designing for most major Australian theatre and opera companies. Shaun's connections with Asian theatre include a 1993 invitation to deliver a paper in Tokyo on Australian theatre design. Recent productions include *Sanctuary* and *The Incorruptible* for Playbox and *Arcadia, Private Lives* and *Julius Caesar* for the MTC. Theatre awards include Green Room Awards for *Steaming, Rivers of China* and *Masterclass*. From 1990 to 1994, Shaun was Associate Director/Designer of the State Theatre Company of South Australia and in 1994, held the position of Festival Designer for the Adelaide Festival of Arts.

REBECCA HEADLAM
ASSISTANT DIRECTOR

Rebecca is the recipient of an Australia Council Development Grant enabling her to join Playbox as Assistant Director for both *Competitive Tenderness* and *Strangers in the Night*. Earlier this year Rebecca trained as a director at Charles Sturt University. Her directing credits include *Strings* (Sydney Fringe Festival) and *Minimum Wage* (Performance Space Sydney and Backspace Theatre Royal, Hobart). She has worked as Assistant Director on *The Rover* at MTC, *Comedy of Errors* at Zootango Theatre Company and *Death and the Maiden* at WBK Theatre in Canberra.

MONICA MAUGHAN
ACTOR

Monica is a highly respected and multi-award winning stage, television and film actor. Her credits include *A Whip Round for Percy Grainger, Long Day's Jorney into Night* and *The Secret House* for Playbox. She has a long association with the MTC appearing in such shows as *Old Times, Loot, Kid Stakes, Gulls, The Importance of Being Earnest, My Father's Father, A Cheery Soul* and *The Last Yankee*. Her extensive television credits include *Prisoner, Flying Doctors, Col'n Carpenter* and *The Damnation of Harvey McHugh* and a *Close Ups* episode for the ABC. Her film credits include *The Getting of Wisdom, Annie's Coming Out, Cactus, A Woman's Tale* and *Road to Nhill.*

MARNIE McDONALD
STAGE MANAGER

A graduate of Swinburne University, Marnie's recent theatre credits include *My Father's Father* and *Julius Ceasar* for MTC, *Dante Through the Invisible* and *Viva La Vida! Frida Kahlo* for Handspan, *The Supper* for Stable Productions, *Buddha – The Light of Asia, Bodhisattva, Odissi: The Sensuous Spirit* and *The Churning Ocean* for the Bharatam Dance Company, *Skins* for St Martins Youth Arts Centre, *Electric Diva* and *Malache* for Arena and *Pacific Union* for Playbox.

SIMON PALOMARES
ACTOR

Simon studied Drama and Psychology at Rusden State College and has since had a varied career as an actor, writer and director in theatre, television and radio. His most well known role was in the show *Wogs Out of Work* which he also wrote and produced. He performed in two other shows *Give Me a Break, The Monte Carlos* and *Tiboldi Brothers* which he also wrote. Simon's theatre credits include *When She Danced, Hysteria* and *The Rover* for MTC, *Hit and Run* and *Snag.* Television credits include *Snowy, Boys from the Bush, Skirts, Mission Impossible, The Man from Snowy River* and *Acropolis Now.* Film credits include *The Lighthorsemen* and the Spanish/American production, *Shooting Elizabeth.*

RICHARD PIPER
ACTOR

Richard is a well established theatre, television and film actor and music performer in Australia and Europe. He has done a string of West End shows including *Grease* and *Elvis*. He has also toured the world for five years with the rock band The Bouncing Czecks. His Australian theatre credits include *The New Rocky Horror Show* and *Moby Dick*. For Playbox he performed in *Picasso at the Lapin Agile* and *A Happy and Holy Occasion*. For MTC he appeared in *A Flea in Her Ear, Someone Who'll Watch Over Me, As You Like It, The Importance of Being Earnest* and *The Recruiting Officer* among many others. Australian and UK television credits include *Correlli, Blue Heelers, Secrets, House Rules, Coronation Street, The Battlers, Minder* and *Fable*, to be shown next year.

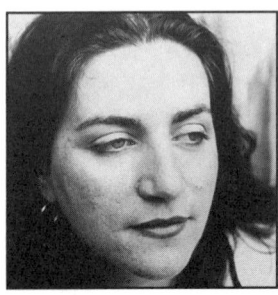 

EFTERPI SOROPOS
LIGHTING DESIGNER

Effie has designed for the Canberra Theatre Company, the National Festival of Theatre, Belvoir Street, Sydney Theatre Company, The Performance Space, Kickhouse Theatre, Chamber Made Opera, Melbourne Workers' Theatre and the Sydney Gay and Lesbian Mardi Gras. Effie also works on dance festival performances in Vancouver, Montreal, Calgary and Hong Kong.

DORIS YOUNANE
ACTOR

Doris graduated from NIDA in 1986 and has since established herself as a theatre, film and television actor. She has worked as a choreographer and trained as a flying trapeze artist with the French flying school, Jean Palacy. Her theatre credits include *Medea, Blabbermouth, Dags, Away, The Tempest, A Midsummer Night's Dream, Les Liaisons Dangereuses* and *A Winter's Tale*. Television credits include *GP, All Together Now, Embassy, Secrets, Us and Them* and *Heartbreak High*. Film credits include *Evil Angels, Death in Brunswick, Resistance* and *The Heartbreak Kid*.

PLAYBOX WRITERS' SUPPORT PROGRAM

Playbox's Writers' Support Program is a vital part of the company's operations.

Each year, hundreds of Australian scripts including entries for the Playbox/Asialink Playwriting Competition and commissions come to the company for assessment. All plays receive feedback and many plays are guided through several drafts; some receive extensive dramaturgical development and workshopping, some are included in Playbox's Theatre in the Raw series of works in progress and others advance to the stage in the company's subscription season.

Playbox co-ordinates with other Australian theatre companies - as well as with developmental companies such as Stages (WA), Playworks (NSW), Playlab (QLD) and the Australian National Playwrights' Centre - and co-operates with them in workshops and co-productions.

Playbox is proud of its support of Australian writers and the role it takes as Australia's leading contemporary theatre company. Many companies now look to Playbox to undertake this crucial development work before including new Australian plays in their own seasons.

Australian playwrights currently under commission from Playbox:

Kim Carpenter	Johann McIntyre
Matt Cameron	Joanna Murray-Smith
Raimondo Cortese	Louis Nowra
Murray Copland	Tom Petsinis
Barry Dickins	Abe Pogos
Jodi Gallagher	Hannie Rayson
Howard Griffith	John Romeril
Rodney Hall	Deidre Rubenstein
Kevin Harrington	Peter Anthony Ryan
Daniel Keene	Peter Scriven
Margaret Kirby	Stephen Sewell
Laura Lattuada	Alana Valentine
Daniel Lillford	Evan Watts
Adam May	Linden Wilkinson

The 1996 Playbox Writers' Support Program is assisted by the Literature Board of the Australia Council.

Principal sponsors:

HOLDING REDLICH
LAWYERS AND CONSULTANTS

Mr and Mrs G Anderson	Ms M Brereton	Mr P Martin
Mr and Mrs J Cain	Ms J Griggs	Ms J Stellato-Pledger
Mr R Peters	Ms H Shardey	
Mrs S St John	Mrs V Brass	

PLAYBOX THEATRE CENTRE OF MONASH UNIVERSITY

THE ⑮ MALTHOUSE

Grant Street Traffic Closure

To enable work to begin on the Melbourne City Link project, Grant Street will be closed to all traffic between St Kilda Road and Sturt Street from April 1996.

Transfield-Obayashi, the joint venture contracted by Transurban to design and construct the project, requires access to Grant Street for the construction of two tunnels under the Domain and Yarra River to link the West Gate Freeway and the South-Eastern Arterial. Pedestrian access will be maintained alongside the Victorian College of the Arts and will be lit at night.

Grant Street will be closed to traffic until the tunnels are scheduled to open by the year 2000. Grant Street at Dodds Street will be redesigned at the completion of construction as a pedestrian precinct with its design reflecting the surrounding Arts Precinct.

Playbox will advise patrons of further developments as news comes to hand.

1996 CURRENCY PRESS CURRENT THEATRE SERIES

THE BLACK SEQUIN DRESS
Jenny Kemp
In the style of performance art, Jenny Kemp explores the extraordinary resonances of ordinary action.
ISBN 0 86819 466 2

BURNING TIME
Nicholas Flanagan
A compelling portrait of a talented, affluent Melbourne family and their friends. Beneath the glittering fun is a heartfelt cry. ISBN 0 86819 464 6

EMMA
Graham Pitts
Pitts' adaptation of the autobiography of Emma Ciccotosto is a celebration of love, life and all things Italian. ISBN 0 86819 467 0

GARY'S HOUSE
Debra Oswald
What begins as a satire becomes a moving drama about a group of battlers trying to turn a dream into reality.
ISBN 0 86819 465 4

JERUSALEM
Michael Gurr
This is a play about the dangers of trying to do good – and public versus private morality. An unusual love story, told with humour, insight and subtlety.
ISBN 0 86819 463 8

THE MOURNING AFTER
Verity Laughton
Fading radio star, Belle Doyle, searches through her memories and mementoes, dissecting her life with wicked humour.
ISBN 0 86819 461 1

NIGHT ON BALD MOUNTAIN
Patrick White
Dark poetry explores the heart and the intellect in a study of misplaced love and desire. ISBN 0 86819 469 7

STRANGERS IN THE NIGHT
Abe Pogos
A contemporary thriller which explores the fascination and fear evoked by the city which never sleeps. ISBN 0 86819 462 X

THE TORRENTS
Oriel Gray
When Rufus Torrent, owner of the *Koolgalla Argus,* employs a new assistant editor J.G. Milford and the 'J' turns out to stand for Jenny, it's more than a gold mining town in the 1890s can bear.
ISBN 0 86819 471 9

THE VENETIAN TWINS
Terence Clarke and Nick Enright
A musical comedy of love and errors set on a single day somewhere between Verona and Jindyworobak.
ISBN 0 86819 474 3

When you've got the tradition,
the pride and the spirit it shows
in everything you do

Carlton. One of the world's great brewers.
CUB proudly supporting Playbox Theatre Company.

[BRIAN *stalks towards her. She stops him, coquettishly.*]
Brian, remember what we talked about? Not at work. So this is my proposal, darling. Are you listening?
BRIAN: I suppose so.
DAWN: What we do is that we transfer nearly all of the money we spend on community services and we put it into vehicle maintenance, over here.
BRIAN: Why would we do that Dawn?
DAWN: Because that's already been tendered pet. And that way, we make our target of fifty percent of all expenditure, by mid next year. And that way, the headmaster will be very pleased with us.
BRIAN: He might even make us head prefects.
DAWN: He might.
BRIAN: But darling there's only one catch.
DAWN: What's that darling?
BRIAN: We don't need to spend ten million dollars on vehicle maintenance.
DAWN: Oh I think we do Brian. I think the car is a symbol in this society. A symbol of success and financial stability and I think the people of Greater Burke will feel duly proud.
BRIAN: But what about Community Services?
DAWN: What about them?
BRIAN: We can't just stop them. I mean that's a fundamental part of our role in local government.
DAWN: It was pet. It was. But we simply can't afford that sort of largess any more. I mean it's nice to be able to help people Brian. I understand that. I was in the Girl Guides.
BRIAN: Oh were you Dawn. I was in the Scouts.
DAWN: I know. You've told me. Many times. So we both know Brian how good it feels to be involved with charity. But just because it makes us feel all warm and fuzzy inside, that doesn't mean it's the responsible course of action. In this instance.
BRIAN: I see your point.
[DAWN *drapes herself provocatively over the desk.*]
DAWN: I knew you would.
[BRIAN *runs a finger along the inside of her leg.* DAWN *responds similarly. There is a knock at the door.* BRIAN *leaps*

away. DAWN *finds herself standing on her desk.* DELIA *enters.*
She is also wearing the regulation red suit.]

DELIA: You wanted to see me?

DAWN: Yes, Delia. Thank you. Just letting a bit of fresh air in. Bit stuffy in here, don't you find.

BRIAN: I'll just ... um.

DAWN: Good idea Brian. If you do that, then I'll do the ... um other thing.

[BRIAN *exits.* DAWN *climbs down and wheels out her white board. We hear the background noise of a street demonstration coming through the open window.*]

Delia, in management discourse, we sometimes use a graph to understand the forces in society that pull people in different directions.

[*She draws the graph as in Act One.*]

Oh that racket! Hells bells! Down here in the south-east quadrant we have the type of person that we call "The Survivor" or "Conscript" and in my opinion that's the type of person Amelia is. "The Conscript" is the type of person who's a plodder basically. No real creativity or initiative. And that's why I've put Amelia in Reception.

[*From outside the noise level increases. We hear the chant: "What do we want? Jobs! When do we want them? Now!"*]

Oh I have to do something about this. Sorry Delia.

[*She clambers up onto her filing cabinet and leans out the window.*]

[*Shouting*] Piss off, you lazy bludgers. Go on. Go and get a job. And to you too.

[*She shuts the window abruptly, just as a rotten tomato smashes against the pane. The noise is much reduced.*]

Ah. That's better. Now where was I? Up here in the north-west, we have what we call "The Activator". The type of person who engages with people and really motivates them. And that's where I put you Delia. Up here. Now as you know in the new organisational structure, I've collapsed several departments into one and I now find I've got a vacancy for the position of Manager of Community Services. I'd like to offer it to you.

DELIA: Manager of Community Services? That's an A2 job. Are you serious?

DAWN: Deadly serious.

DELIA: But ... I don't know that I've got the skills to oversee that size budget. I mean we're looking at an annual budget of around ten million, aren't we?

DAWN: No. No. Community Services has taken a bit of a cut. We're talking around the twenty-five thousand mark. Notwithstanding, it's a very responsible portfolio and I happen to think you're eminently qualified to take it on.

[*There is a knock at the door.*]

Come in.

[AMELIA *enters.*]

Yes Amelia?

AMELIA: I've got that information for you.

DAWN: What information Milly?

AMELIA: You know. 'Bout the ... You know.

[*She nods towards* DELIA *and tries to suggest in mime,* DELIA*'s boyfriend.*]

DAWN: Oh I see. The information about the ... oh yes.

AMELIA: I'll put it here will I?

DAWN: Thank you Milly.

[AMELIA *exits.*]

DELIA: She's such a conscript.

DAWN: Oh Milly?

AMELIA: Yes.

DAWN: Milly I have to pop out for a moment.

AMELIA: Well don't be long. Mr Farkley and Mr Ricotto are going to be here any minute.

DAWN: I'm sure Delia will be happy to entertain them. Won't you Delia? If I'm a bit late.

SCENE FIVE

Staff lunch room.

KEL *walks in and sits down.* PIGGY *immediately turns his back.* PIGGY, *appointed now as Assistant Dog Catcher is sneezing and snuffling. He looks the picture of misery.*

KEL: How you going Pig?
  [*Silence.*]
TREV: He caught his first dog today.
KEL: Really. Good on yer.
  [*Silence.*]
PIGGY: I'm allergic to dog hair.
KEL: Ah. Well how's everyone?
  [*No-one speaks.*]
  Delia? Cat got your tongue?
DELIA: I don't talk to scabs.
KEL: Oh come on. Who was it that got him the job as Assistant Dog
  Catcher eh? Who went to see Dawn Snow to make sure he didn't
  get the boot? Eh? Delia?
DELIA: Sure Kel, you're a great bloke.
  [*Silence.* MERLE *enters.*]
  Merle! I've been trying to call you.
MERLE: Hi all.
DELIA: Can I have a word?
MERLE: Sure.
AMELIA [*P.A. announcement in the lunchroom*]: Delia. Delia
  Kibbitrawhib to Reception please. Mr Farkley's here.
DELIA: Oh shit!
  [DELIA *leaps into the toilet and closes the door. She re-opens
  it.*]
  I'm not here alright.
  [*Recloses it.*]
MERLE: Delia. What's going on? Delia. Let me in.
  [*She bangs incessantly until* DELIA *opens the door and lets*
  MERLE *in.* BRIAN *enters.*]
BRIAN: Anyone seen Merle?
TREV: She's in the toilet with Delia.
BRIAN: Ah. Right.
P.A.: Delia. Delia to Reception please.
BRIAN [*tapping*]: Um Delia. Excuse me Delia. Um ... sorry 'bout
  this. Delia?
  [DELIA *and* MERLE *come out of the toilet.*]
MERLE: Go on. Do it. Afternoon, Brian. You can do it.
DELIA: Do I have to?

70

MERLE: Yes!
  [DELIA *exits.*]
  Brian do you know what that Snow woman's done now?
BRIAN: What's that Merle?
MERLE: She's cut the Community Services budget by nine million dollars.
BRIAN: Oh surely not. There must be some mistake.
MERLE: Brian. I want her sacked. This is the last straw. I'm going to call an extraordinary meeting and demand that she's removed from office. This is too much.

SCENE SIX

Reception.
DELIA *approaches* FARKLEY *and* ROCKO *with her hand outstreched.*

DELIA: Mr Farkley. Mr Ricotto. Delia Kibbitrawhib.
ROCKO: Hello.
FARKLEY: Delia.
DELIA: Oh "Deals". Please. Everybody calls me "Deals".
  Would you like to come through. Mrs Snow won't be long.
  [*They exit.*]

SCENE SEVEN

BRIAN, *in full mayoral regalia ushers two* ELDERLY WOMEN *and a press* PHOTOGRAPHER *into the Reception area.*

BRIAN: What about just here. In front of the Queen. [*Photo*]
MRS GILLESPIE.: Ooh, that sounds nice.
BRIAN: Perhaps I could stand in the middle and these two lovely ladies could stand on either side.
MRS RANDALL: Yes. That sounds nice.

PHOTOGRAPHER: Yeah. Um. What's this for again? My editor didn't give me any details.

BRIAN: This is for the Burke Annual Art Show, Gerry. An annual event at our Neighbourhood House which gives great pleasure to a lot of people in Greater Burke. Mrs Gillespie here has won first prize for her china painting.

[MRS GILLESPIE *holds up her winning plate.*]

And Mrs Randall won first prize in ... um ... knitting.

MRS RANDALL: Macrame.

[MRS RANDALL *holds up her macrame. They form a smiling tableau.*]

PHOTOGRAPHER: Oh yeah. That's good. Hold that.

[*Suddenly* DAWN *bursts in. The noise of the demonstration blares through the open door. "Farkley Out! Farkley Out!" is chanted by the demonstrators. Rotten fruit is pelted into the Town Hall.*]

DAWN [*calls out aggressively*]: Repulsive scum! That's what you are. Human filth!

[*She gives the crowd the finger.*]

Up yours too.

[*She slams the door and turns to find the press* PHOTOGRAPHER *snapping pictures of her and* BRIAN *and his artists staring agape.*]

Oh. Some people. Goodness me. Even with something as devastating as unemployment your ordinary Australian still has an indomitable spirit eh? Laugh? Goodness me. All the fun of a children's party out there.

[*The* PHOTOGRAPHER *keeps snapping.* DAWN *realises the implications.*]

Excuse me. What do you think you're doing?

BRIAN: Dawn! This is Gerry. He's a press photographer.

DAWN: Really? How do you do Gerry.

[DAWN *makes as if to shake his hand. She grabs his camera and removes the film.*]

PHOTOGRAPHER: Hey! What are you doing?

[*He snatches the camera back.* DAWN *grabs it again.*]

DAWN: Sorry Gerry, no photographs without permission. You're contravening The Town Hall Photo Act, Section 3, Paragraph 6.

BRIAN [*dismayed*]: Dawn, that was –

DAWN: Brian, really!
　　[*She exits.*]

SCENE EIGHT

DAWN's *office.*
DAWN *enters to find* DELIA, FARKLEY *and* ROCKO *waiting.*

DAWN: Oh! Mr Farkley. What a pleasure. And Rocko. Goodness
　　me. I'm so sorry I'm a bit tardy. It's a nightmare out there, isn't
　　it? Heavens above. All that shouting, "Farkley Out! Farkley
　　Out!" Really. If I had my way, I'd firebomb the lot of them.
　　[DAWN *tinkles with anxious laughter.*]
　　Anyway, I'm sure you were in good hands. You've had a cup of
　　tea, have you?
FARKLEY: Yes. Yes, Deals's been looking after us.
DAWN: Deals? Good. Has Deals mentioned her new job? Manager
　　of Community Services.
FARKLEY: Yes.
DAWN: I've just promoted her.
FARKLEY: Yes.
ROCKO: And given Community Services an injection of six million
　　dollars I believe.
DAWN: I beg your pardon?
FARKLEY: Deals has been telling us how committed you are to
　　expanding the welfare program here.
DELIA: Mrs Snow. Just hold still. I think you've got something in
　　your hair. Ah! Got it.
DAWN: What is it?
DELIA: Um ... a piece of tomato I think.
DAWN: I think that might be all now, Delia. Thank you. Sixteen
　　million dollars is not quite the same as managing the petty cash
　　is it? No. Not when our primary focus is delivering up the
　　savings. Which of course is what we're all interested in.
FARKLEY: Well, not all together, Mrs Snow.

DAWN: No, not all together. But in fairly sizeable instalments. Of course. Thank you Delia. Off you pop.

FARKLEY: Well it's been very interesting to hear about this new direction. [*Stands*] Deals, it's been a pleasure.

DAWN: Um ... what direction is that Deals?

DELIA [*ignoring her*]: Oh, the pleasure's mine. Mr Farkley. Believe me. Rocko. Mrs Snow. [*To* FARKLEY] Bye. For now.
[*She drifts out.*]

FARKLEY: Charming girl.

DAWN: Yes. Charming.

FARKLEY: Full of good ideas too.

DAWN: Yes. Full to brimming.

FARKLEY: Mrs Snow. As you know in the past four years the culture of this state has turned full circle.

DAWN: Hasn't it just. A complete circle. The full 350 degrees.
[*Beat.*]

FARKLEY: Three hundred ... Yes. The state budget's returned to surplus and now of course we're moving towards a Triple A credit rating.

DAWN: And it's a credit to you. that's all I can say. Golly gosh. Triple A. Marvellous. And I for one, am proud, truly proud to be a person living and working –

ROCKO: Mrs Snow.

DAWN: Yes?

FARKLEY: The point, Mrs Snow is that now confidence has been restored, we are in a position to turn our attention to the social fabric. Because the rewards of a stable economic framework can begin to flow.

DAWN: Well I am very committed – if I may speak, Mr Ricotto – to the flow. Go with the flow. I've always said it. Go with the flow and if it flows into the um social thingo – excellent. Couldn't be better.

FARKLEY: No doubt your experience in Uganda –

DAWN: Precisely. In fact my extensive experience in the prison system, has made it possible for me to secure the services of several men, on the early release scheme from Pentridge to take up employment here as Parking Officers.

FARKLEY: Really.

74

DAWN: Yes. I spoke to Mr Smilevski – Actually speaking of things Macedonian, I feel I have to say the comments in the press from Mrs Merle Pickhaver –

ROCKO: Who?

[*They both repeat the laughing routine as in Act One.*]

FARKLEY: Speaking of Mrs Pickhaver.

DAWN: Oh do we have to.

[*All three laugh conspiratorially.*]

So uncalled for I thought. I mean I shouldn't really be telling tales out of school, but honest to goodness The Macedonian Community can't abide the woman.

FARKLEY: Really?

ROCKO: But she's the chair of the building committee for the new Macedonian Cultural Centre.

DAWN: Under sufferance, let me tell you. But far be it for me to criticise, when she is, after all, my employer.

FARKLEY: Indeed. So you have connections do you, Mrs Snow, with the Macedonian community?

DAWN: Oh connections! Mr Farkley. I am so connected that I'm ... well I am a Macedonian. I mean I'm British, well a British Australian, of course but inside, inside my heart I'm Macedonian. Through and through.

[*She waves her handkerchief in the air and hums a traditional Macedonian folksong.*]

FARKLEY: Mrs Snow. Can I be frank with you?

DAWN: Mr Farkley, I wouldn't want it any other way. Please. Be as frank as you wish.

FARKLEY: Mrs Snow, this is a very delicate matter, but the fact is, Mrs Pickhaver's activities are quite frankly causing some consternation amongst certain people in the government. She's been very outspoken on a range of issues: local government reform, our Youth/Family Program and now this latest business with the Macedonians and Diversity Management –

ROCKO: Which she knows nothing about.

DAWN: Oh absolutely nothing. It's appalling. Completely ignorant. And what's worse, the press is giving her so much air play and these are all your portfolios. She clearly has no concern for your feelings whasoever.

FARKLEY: None.

DAWN: Tsch. Ghastly, insensitive woman. That's all I can say. And apart from her appalling dress sense –

ROCKO: Appalling.

FARKLEY: Appalling!

DAWN: She is standing in the way of everything that we are trying to do here in Greater Burke.

ROCKO: Scandalous.

DAWN: In fact if I were in your shoes Mr Farkley I'd have to restrain myself from –

ROCKO: Putting her up against the wall?

DAWN: Getting rid of her, Mr Ricotto. Goodbye Mrs Pickhaver. And good riddens.

FARKLEY: Yes, but of course one has to curtail one's own feelings in this matter, Mrs Snow.

DAWN: Of course one does Mr Farkley.

FARKLEY: Even though one knows that the people of Greater Burke are suffering.

DAWN: Oh they are.

FARKLEY: But that's democracy Mrs Snow.

DAWN: Yes, so flawed. But it is all we have, after all.

FARKLEY: Of course I would never intervene in the democratic process –

DAWN: No.

FARKLEY: Because I believe in it Mrs Snow.

DAWN: I know you do. You're a shining example to us.

FARKLEY: But of course if the Council were to be grossly incompetent at any stage, I would have to intervene and sack them all. I mean not the Executive of course.

DAWN: No. We are doing our best after all. Under very trying circumstances. Um ... with Council. Not with the government.

FARKLEY: No. But I would have to intervene. There would be no other course of action.

DAWN: No. No. There wouldn't. So what sort of things Mr Farkley would you say might constitute "gross incompetence"? I mean hypothetically speaking, what would be grossly incompetent *enough*, if you see what I mean?

FARKLEY: Oh I do Mrs Snow.

DAWN: If we didn't meet our CCT target?

FARKLEY: Well that would be unacceptable.

DAWN: Unacceptable enough?

FARKLEY: That would be against the law.

ROCKO: And then there's the leaking of confidential information.

DAWN: Oh gross!

FARKLEY: Very gross.

ROCKO: Like the fact that we're going to have to cut all funding to the Youth Arts Festival.

DAWN: Oh gross. I mean if that were to get out. Highly sensitive information.

ROCKO: Oh quite. Of course we wouldn't want to see the Executive implicated in any incompetence, Mrs Snow.

DAWN: No we would not.

ROCKO: We'd want to be sure that the debt was under control, for example, and all efforts had been made to sell assets, that sort of thing.

DAWN: Well isn't that funny you should mention assets, Mr Ricotto. Because I just happen to have a very interested party in purchasing a rather large tract of Council land, which quite frankly is not much use to anyone. So we're moving ahead on that one.

FARKLEY: Excellent. Clearly the people of Greater Burke have one asset which none of us want to get rid of.

DAWN: What is that Mr Farkley?

FARKLEY: Their Chief Executive Officer.

DAWN: Oh, Mr Farkley.

FARKLEY: Oh, Mrs Snow.

SCENE NINE

Reception.
BRIAN *hastens to catch* DAWN *as she is waving goodbye to* ROCKO *and* FARKLEY.

BRIAN [*breathlessly*]: Dawn. Oh Dawn. I have to talk to you. In private. Something terrible's come up.

DAWN: Bye. Ta ra. What Brian? Cheerio.

BRIAN: Merle's plotting against you Dawn.

DAWN: Ciao. What are you talking about Brian?

BRIAN: She's called a secret meeting of Council. She wants to sack you.

DAWN: Oh does she. Why is that Brian?

BRIAN: Because you've slashed the Community Services budget. She's hopping mad Dawn.

DAWN: Excuse me, Brian. [*To* AMELIA] Amelia, that report on my desk that details my proposal to inject a further six million dollars into Community Services. Could you make eight copies and distribute them by courier to the Councillors private homes please.

AMELIA: Certainly, Mrs Snow.

BRIAN: But what about the CCT target?

DAWN: Oh that old furphy. It's a paper tiger Brian. Mr Farkley's not concerned. His main interest is in delivering the best possible services to the people of Greater Burke. Social fabric, you know. All that.

AMELIA: Excuse me Mrs Snow. Why only eight copies? There are nine Councillors.

DAWN: Yes. Don't worry about Mrs Pickhaver. She doesn't really need one.

BRIAN: Oh Dawn. That's not fair.

DAWN: Brian, I think Mrs Pickhaver needs an opportunity to clear the air. Get all her concerns about me off her chest. And then of course, the other Councillors can have the chance to tell her just how misinformed and ignorant she is. I think that will be liberating for everyone. Don't you feel?

SCENE TEN

FARKLEY: Why did you want to leak that information about the Youth Arts Festival?

ROCKO: Well that's pretty harmless isn't it? We just start a little disturbance about something like that. Take the heat off the hospital issue.

FARKLEY: Right.

ROCKO: Then we can bow to community pressure and re-instate the funding to the Youth Arts Festival.

FARKLEY: Right. The people have to feel they've got some power in these matters.

ROCKO: Exactly.

FARKLEY: Meanwhile we have to take a hard line on Councillors leaking confidential information.

ROCKO: I think so.

FARKLEY: That's just totally unacceptable.

ROCKO: Totally.

SCENE ELEVEN

Reception.

DAWN: Milly, can you pop this on the courier to Merle Pickhaver. This is the covering letter to my Community Services proposal and then if you could just pop this in the envelope with it.

AMELIA: Sure.

DAWN: Thanks.

AMELIA: Oh Mrs Snow.

DAWN: What Milly?

AMELIA: Um ... this is a memo to you. From Mr Farkley.

DAWN: Oh really?

AMELIA: It's about a proposal to cut funds to the Youth Arts Festival. Strictly private and confidential.

DAWN: Oh dear. I must have made a mistake.
   [*She turns her back and seals the envelope.*]
   Just as well you're on the ball, Milly.

SCENE TWELVE

DAWN, BRIAN *and* AMELIA *sit around the desk.*

DAWN: Brian you don't mind if Amelia sits in on this meeting do you?

BRIAN: Not at all.

DAWN: She's volunteered very kindly to take notes.

BRIAN: Ah. Jolly good.

DAWN: You see I have big things in mind for Amelia. I'm grooming her. I'm hoping that one day Amelia might become my personal assistant.
   [AMELIA *smiles happily. During the course of the conversation she is careful to imitate* DAWN'*s gestures, crossing and uncrossing her legs at the same time etc.*]

BRIAN: As long as this doesn't interfere with Amelia's other work. For Council.

DAWN: Not at all. Amelia is very committed to professional development and training. She's sought me out as something of a mentor. Which I'm very happy to be. Especially when someone shows that kind of initiative. *Volunteering* to do her other work outside hours.

AMELIA: Outside hours?

DAWN: Only when necessay. You see, too often Amelia, people in my position, very senior accomplished people just pull the ladder up behind them. But not me. Because I believe in nurturing the young.

AMELIA: I know.

DAWN: With kindness, patience and at times discipline. Not that I'm that much older, really. I just seem to have risen up, lightly and quickly.

AMELIA: Like a souffle. Um. No.

DAWN: No.

BRIAN: Hard work and discipline Amelia. That's the ticket.

DAWN: And one other thing. What's the magic ingredient? Remember? Milly?

AMELIA [posturing]: Flair.

DAWN: Lovely. Oh isn't she going to be lovely Brian?

BRIAN: Lovely.

DAWN: Now. Brian, I've just had a word with the Minister –

BRIAN: The Minister?

DAWN: Yes. The Minister. And it has come to his notice that we haven't delivered the rate reductions, at this stage. Nor have we managed to nibble too far into our little debt problem. In fact we could be looking down the barrel at the "B" word.

BRIAN: What's the "B" word?

DAWN: "B" stands for Brian and coincidentally it also stands for Bankrupcy. And it does occur to me that the two are somewhat interconnected.

BRIAN: Bankrupcy!

DAWN: As you can appreciate Brian, in your first term as Mayor, this is not going to look good.

BRIAN: Oh Dawn. I'm devastated. I ... um –

DAWN: Yes well you'll be more devastated I promise if this gets out. Of course I could say to the press that all blame rests with the previous administration, but I suspect you may fare rather badly, given –

BRIAN: Yes.

DAWN: Albeit unfairly.

BRIAN: Quite.

AMELIA: Sorry, I missed that. Why would Brian fare badly?

DAWN: Because Brian was involved in the previous administration.

AMELIA: Deputy Mayor?

DAWN: Mm.

AMELIA: D'you know what I was in a previous administration? I was Emmeline Pankhurst.

81

DAWN: Extraordinary. Brian, I do think that there may be a solution.

BRIAN: A solution. Good. We need a solution.

AMELIA: I chained myself to a pillar box –

DAWN: We have to consider asset sales Brian. And I think sooner rather than later.

BRIAN: But Dawn we have no real assets. This is the problem.

AMELIA: And when they dragged me off to prison, I starved. In protest.

DAWN: We do have an asset Brian, a very significant one –

AMELIA: I starved until I was weak –

DAWN: Shut up for Chrissake. Brian, I'm referring to the land which is currently languishing under the Neighbourhood House.

BRIAN: Oh Dawn.

DAWN: Council owned and currently costing us a great deal of money which we can ill afford to spend.

BRIAN: But Dawn that's a community facility. We can't sell that.

DAWN: So is electricity, Brian but we sold that.

AMELIA: And we still have the light.

DAWN: That's right.

BRIAN: Oh it's out of the question. The Council wouldn't stand for it. And neither would the community. I'm sorry Dawn but it's not an option. I must stand firm on this.

DAWN: Milly make an appointment with the editor of the Burke Standard please.

BRIAN: Oh Dawn, please.

DAWN: Go on, Milly. Do it now. I think it's important the public are kept informed.

[AMELIA *stands.*]

BRIAN: Amelia. Please. Just a minute. Sit down

[DAWN *stands.*]

Dawn, listen, there must be some other alternative.

DAWN [*shouting*]: There is no alternative. You are sending us bankrupt Brian. And for what? For the sake of a few old ladies doing china painting.

BRIAN: Dawn. It's more than that.

[*She turns on him.*]

DAWN: What more can it possibly be? It's an ugly house in an ugly street. It doesn't even have period features. It's nothing more than an eyesore, to anyone with an ounce of aesthetic. And very soon Brian they'll be writing more of their infernal submissions. For capital works, this time. A new kitchen. Faulty plumbing. Re-wiring, re-stumping. Some sort of vulgar extension, so the play group have got more space to run amuck and flick paint at each other. But what's another hundred thousand dollars Brian. Since we've got so much money to throw around.

[DAWN *bursts into tears.*]

BRIAN: Oh Dawn. Amelia, tissue please.

[AMELIA *leaps to her feet and leaves the room.* BRIAN *moves over to* DAWN.]

DAWN: What do you think you're doing?

BRIAN: Oh Dawnie.

DAWN: I said, don't. Don't even think about it. I forbid you to touch any part of my body.

BRIAN: Dawn.

DAWN: Don't call me that.

BRIAN: What shall I call you then?

[DAWN *ignores him.*]

Let me talk to Merle. I'm sure that um ... together we'll come up with something.

DAWN: I hope so Brian. I really hope so.

[*She sweeps out the door into her own office and slams the door.* AMELIA *returns with tissues, a glass of water and a pill.* BRIAN *takes it and swallows, mopping his brow with the tissues.*]

AMELIA: Hey. That was for Dawn.

BRIAN: Don't call her that.

SCENE THIRTEEN

BRIAN's *office.*
BRIAN *is in a meeting with* MERLE.

MERLE: No way. I'm sorry Brian. That is one of the most valued community facilities we've got. No way.

BRIAN: But Merle what you have to understand is that we have no alternative.

MERLE: Bullshit Brian. She's cranking up this business about the debt, purely to make us look like we've mismanaged our affairs.

BRIAN: Why would she do that?

MERLE: To make herself look like she is the great white hope. Which she is not.

BRIAN: I don't think so Merle. The evidence is there in the draft budget.

MERLE: Which Council won't approve Brian. Can't you see? She's set impossible targets, just so she can suck up to that little nerd Farkley.

BRIAN: Oh Dawn wouldn't do that.

MERLE: Brian, she wants Greater Burke to be the model Council.

BRIAN: Don't we all Merle.

MERLE: But not that kind of model Brian. That's the difference. We want Greater Burke to be a great place to live. A place where people are cared for and helped. People out there feel proud of our traditions Brian. They stay here and they grow old here. This is not just a stepping stone to moving on into some swankier suburb. They see themselves as Burke people. And they think about this Town Hall as being a symbol. A symbol that articulates a kind of pride in who they are and where they've come from.

BRIAN: I knew that.

MERLE: Dawn Snow wants to institute a program that will destroy everything we've set up, just so she can prove she's capable of delivering up the savings. Which is the only thing Farkley's interested in.

BRIAN: Look I don't want to sell the Neighbourhood House any more than you do. But the problem is quite frankly, it's a big drain on Council funds.

MERLE: What?

BRIAN: Um. Very soon I'm sure we're going to get submissions for capital works. A new kitchen. New plumbing. Re-wiring, re-stumping. Some sort of extension, and so on. And we'll be talking about another hundred thousand dollars. And where are we going to find that kind of money Merle?

MERLE: Brian, I'm on the management committee. I'd know if there was any talk about capital works.

BRIAN: I'm just not sure that Council can continue to be associated with the sort of largess that some community organisations have come to expect from us. These are of course much straightened times for us all. The Nineties. And we're not just talking about belt tightening Merle. We're talking about stomach stapling.

MERLE: Brian.

BRIAN: Yes Merle.

MERLE: I have a rather uncomfortable feeling that you are being unduly influenced by the views of our CEO.

BRIAN: Not at all.

MERLE: Brian, I'd hate to have to raise the issue of your unsavoury relations with the Chief Executive.

BRIAN: My relations with the Chief Executive are not in the least unsavoury.

[DAWN *knocks and enters.*]

DAWN: Excuse me Brian. Mrs Pickhaver. I believe you wanted to discuss my Neighbourhood House proposition. Is this a good time?

MERLE: Yes.

BRIAN: No. I mean yes. Yes. Why not? Now's as good a time as any? Merle?

MERLE: Yes Mrs Snow. I think now is as good a time as any to discuss what I feel might be a conflict of interest on your part.

DAWN: A conflict of interest?

BRIAN: Ah. Merle. I'm not sure that this is ... um ... appropriate.

MERLE: I think it's perhaps more appropriate than if I raised it at Council, for example.

BRIAN: Merle, I think –

MERLE: It concerns Mr Dragi Smilevski.

BRIAN: Oh. Does it. Jolly good! Yes. I feel it is a more appropriate time to talk about ... um ... him.

DAWN: What about Dragi Smilevski?

MERLE: Mrs Snow, it appears to me that Mr Dragi Smilevski has been faring very well as a result of your appointment. And since it is common knowledge that your family and his family are friends, you have barbeques together on the weekend, that sort of thing –

DAWN: I had a barbeque with Mr Smilevski once, Mrs Pickhaver. Once, when my husband was alive in 1987.

MERLE: But there is a perception, Mrs Snow. A perception, that you are very regular barbeque people. Now whether that is founded in fact I don't know, but I do know that Mr Smilevski won the Traffic tender and now Mr Smilevski wants to buy Neighbourhood House. With your assistance I am presuming.

DAWN: It is correct Mrs Pickhaver that I feel the sale of Neighbourhood House would be a very beneficial thing for Greater Burke. That is correct. Whether Mr Smilevski buys it or anyone else, is of no concern to me. None whatsoever. As long as somebody buys it. Now as to the matter of any conflict of interest, I would draw your attention to a document I've prepared proposing to Council that we abandon our two million dollar capital works program, to establish the Macedonian Cultural Centre.

MERLE: Oh. I'd like to see that document Mrs Snow.

DAWN: First thing tomorrow, Mrs Pickhaver.

MERLE: I'd like to see it now.

DAWN: Sorry. I'm afraid you can't. Sorry.

MERLE: Why not?

DAWN: Because Amelia hasn't finished typing it. And you couldn't possibly read my handwriting. Anyway the point is, the point is Mrs Pickhaver, that if I had any vested interest in Mr Smilevski, who is a Macedonian, I would hardly propose we cut all support to the Macedonian Cultural Centre. Now would I?

BRIAN: No you wouldn't. You definitely wouldn't. I think that's quite clear.

DAWN: Now if you'll excuse me. I have another appointment to attend. With Mr Perelis, who I believe you have had several barbeques with –

MERLE: I have not!

DAWN: Well we shouldn't believe everything we hear should we?

[DAWN *exits*.]

BRIAN: She's got a point Merle. Rumours can be very dangerous.

MERLE: Not as dangerous as the facts Brian, which I would hate to have to unburden to your wife, if it looked as if Neighbourhood House was in jeopardy.

SCENE FOURTEEN

DAWN's *office.*

DAWN: Dragi, as you know I'm totally committed to the sale of Neighbourhood House. And I'd like to give you first option on the purchase.

DRAGI: Dawn, last time we spoke –

DAWN: Last time we spoke was yesterday, Dragi and today is today the first day of the rest of our lives. And as you and I both know we have the future to plan for. With new extensions to be built and big car parks to be developed. Dragi, confidentially there is a lot of resistance to this plan at Council level. So we really have no option but to go higher up and get some help from the Minister.

DRAGI: Kimble Farkley?

DAWN: Yes. Kimble Farkley, who is after all a great champion of the Macedonian community. Now my proposal Dragi is we make an appointment with the Minister to discuss a new initiative which I think will make him very keen to get behind us with the Neighbourhood House sale.

DRAGI: New initiative? What is this?

DAWN: It's a youth employment scheme, Dragi, which you want to run at Smilevski Smallgoods.

DRAGI: I do?

DAWN: You do.

DRAGI: I think I don't.

DAWN: Oh I think you do. And can I tell you why you want to initiate this new scheme?

DRAGI: Please. Tell me. I can't think of one reason myself. Not one.

DAWN: Dragi, you want to set up a new training scheme, in partnership with the state government to get youth on the move off their backsides and into work in this community.

DRAGI: Yes. This is something I definitely do not want to do. Thank you Dawn. Good bye.

DAWN: Dragi! You want the land?

DRAGI: I want the land. I don't want the youth.

DAWN: Youth means land Dragi.

DRAGI: Youth means trouble.

DAWN: Youth means that Smilevski Smallgoods is featured in all the media. Leaders in an impressive community initiative.

DRAGI: Some other scheme Dawn. Not youth. I hate youth.

DAWN: Dragi. Trust me. I don't like young people any more than you do. But it is perfectly possible to have a youth employment program without any youth involved. You know that as well as I do.

DRAGI: What are you talking about?

DAWN: Look at it this way. What young person in their right mind would want to work stuffing dead cow meat into intestines.

DRAGI: That's the trouble with youth. They don't understand hard work. They don't want to get their hands dirty.

DAWN: Precisely. But you tried Dragi. You did your duty as an eminent citizen and businessman to provide opportunities for the young people of this community. And look what happened? No-one, not a single youth availed him or herself of this golden opportunity.

DRAGI: You sure no young person would want to work for me.

DAWN: I'm positive. The only contact you will ever need to have with a young person is when you're posing for the press photographers.

DRAGI: Mmm. I could like this.

DAWN: It's a beautiful idea Dragi. In fact I wish I'd come up with it myself.

DRAGI [*preoccupied*]: I have to stand next to Farkley for these photographs?

DAWN: Of course.

DRAGI: I don't want to stand next to Farkley.

DAWN: Maybe Violetta could stand next to Farkley.

DRAGI: Mmm. No. She doesn't like Farkley.

DAWN: Who would you like to stand next to Dragi? It's completely up to you.

DRAGI: I like to be in the photo, on my own. With Smilevski's in the background.

DAWN: I'll see what I can do.

DRAGI: Yeah. I like that.

DAWN: Farkley will need to get some media coverage too.

DRAGI: Why?

DAWN: Because it was his idea.

DRAGI: No it wasn't. It was my idea.

DAWN: We know that. But you know politicians, Dragi. You have to let them think it was their idea.

[DRAGI *sulks.*]

Dragi?

DRAGI: All right. It was his idea. But I'm not happy.

DAWN: But you will be Dragi. Because very soon Smilevski Smallgoods will be ready to take on the world.

DRAGI: Mmm. Maybe.

DAWN: Don is good, but Smilevski is smarvellous.

SCENE FIFTEEN

In a covered walkway where employees go to have a smoke. MERLE *and* DELIA *are having a cigarette outside, standing next to an overflowing ashtray.*

MERLE: We're going to have to get a big campaign going I reckon.

DELIA: Save the Neighbourhood House.

MERLE: Nothing else will.

DELIA: You know what we need? We need a patron.

[KEL *comes out.*]

KEL: Thought you'd be out here. I heard a whisper about a new job. Any truth in that Delia?

[KEL *lights up. He is ignored.*]

DELIA [*to* MERLE]: I've got it. The Lady Mayoress.

MERLE: Coral?
DELIA: Yep. Coral Guest.
MERLE: But she's an idiot.
DELIA: So is Brian and he's the Mayor.
MERLE: Delia. Brian is pro the sale.
DELIA: And Coral is anti.
MERLE: How do you know?
DELIA: Because I'll tell her she is and Coral loves it when she's got an opinion.
MERLE: Won't she talk to Brian first.
DELIA: I don't think so. They're married. Married people don't do that.
[*They ash their cigarettes and leave.*]

SCENE SIXTEEN

MERLE *and* DELIA *meet* DAWN *in Reception.*

MERLE: Mrs Snow? That report on the Macedonian Cultural Centre? I couldn't find it on my desk this morning.
DAWN: Oh that. Yes. That report. Unfortunately Milly's got RSI. In fact Milly, you really should get that bandaged. Come on in, Milly. Health and safety. Think it. Talk it. Work it.
DELIA: Let's have a look at that Milly?
AMELIA: What?
   [BRIAN *enters.*]
DAWN: No Delia. Best not.
BRIAN: Dawn! Morning Merle. Everyone.
DAWN: Quick sticks Milly.
BRIAN: Guess who I just saw in the carpark?
MERLE: Yassar Arafat?
BRIAN: Kimble Farkley.
   [DAWN *stops in her tracks.*]
   He recognised me of course. And we had a good old chin wag. I think he's rather pleased with the way things are going in Greater Burke. With Council of course.

DAWN: Of course.

BRIAN: In fact I invited him to come and have lunch with me one day at my club.

DAWN: What club is that Brian?

BRIAN: Oh you know. The ol' clubby club. RSL.

AMELIA: That's what I've got. Hurts like buggery too.

DAWN: Yes. Excuse us, if you wouldn't mind.

[*She ushers* AMELIA *into her office.* BRIAN *tags along.*]

BRIAN: They do a very nice roast on a Thursday. We should pop down one time.

[DAWN *closes the door on* BRIAN. *He opens it and keeps talking.*]

See Dawn, forging strong partnerships between state and local government is really the way to go. And I see that as a rather crucial part of my role. In fact I was thinking the mayoral entertainment budget possibly needs a bit of an injection.

[DAWN *is unfurling bandaging from the cupboard.*]

DAWN: What would you like me to inject you with Brian?

BRIAN: Dawn. You do seem a little out of sorts today. Women's problems eh?

DAWN: Brian, has your wife ever told you, you can be a particularly irritating man?

BRIAN: Yes. Yes she has mentioned that.

SCENE SEVENTEEN

BRIAN'*s office*
KEL *bursts in and hands* BRIAN *a piece of paper.*

BRIAN: What's this?

KEL: My resignation.

BRIAN: Oh. I don't actually deal with that Kel. You'll have to see Dawn.

KEL: I'm resigning Brian.

BRIAN: Oh my god. Kel. You can't do that.

KEL: Why not?

BRIAN: Because you are a much valued member of this organisation. You've been with us – how long Kel?

KEL: Twenty-two years.

BRIAN: Twenty-two years. This is unthinkable. This is inconceivable. I cannot stand by and let you do this Kel.

[*The phone rings.*]

Brian Guest. Marty Finkle! How are you? Crikey bob. Marty Finkle. Jeepers creepers. Who'd da thought? Well well well. How are you ol' bean?

[KEL *coughs.*]

Oh. Marty. Marty. Listen. I can't talk. Give me your number and I'll get straight back. Yeah. Right. How's your croquet arm eh? Not bad you ol' bugger. Marty. Speak soon. [*Hangs up.*] Kel, how can I help you?

KEL: You can't. I'm going in there to resign. I've had it Brian.

BRIAN: Oh Kel.

KEL: I can't take it any longer Brian. The Macos hate me and everyone else treats me like scum. I've got no self esteem.

BRIAN: I had that once.

KEL: Really? You've never said anything.

BRIAN: Yeah. Well, it's not the sort of thing you talk about Kel.

KEL: Gee Brian, How'd you get over it?

BRIAN: Dunno. Just went away.

[*Pause.*]

Kel, can I talk to you about something?

KEL: Sure Brian. Anything.

BRIAN: Have you heard anything about myself in connection with Dawn Snow?

KEL: Er, no. Er, what sort of connection are we talking about?

BRIAN: I'm talking about a ... um ... romantic connection.

KEL: Romantic?

BRIAN: Yes.

KEL: No. I've heard nothing about that. I mean I did hear you were porking her –

BRIAN: – Kel! I am not porking Mrs Snow.

KEL: That's what I said. At the staff meeting.

BRIAN: Staff meeting!

KEL: I said Brian wouldn't pork someone like that. I mean let's face it, she's a cow.

BRIAN: Kel. Kel. Stop. Mrs Snow is not a cow. Look. I will admit to you Kelvin, that I have had some feelings of tenderness directed toward Mrs Snow on some occasions.

KEL: Greater Burke let us down badly on Saturday eh? I tell you what, I could have strangled that bloody Gibbo. Dunno why they kept him on the flank. I mean he took a couple of good marks –

BRIAN: – Kel. These feelings that I've been having –

KEL [*song*]: Good ol' Greater Burke forever. They know how to play the game.

BRIAN: I'm thinking of leaving Coral.

KEL [*song*]: Side by side, we stick together.
Coral? Brian. I have to tell you something about Coral.

BRIAN [*excitedly*]: She's having an affair?

KEL: Coral? Come off it. No. Listen. I overheard Merle and Delia talking. They want her to be the patroness of Neighbourhood House.

BRIAN: What?

KEL: They're setting up a Save Neighbourhood House campaign and they want Coral to be the patron.

BRIAN: But that's ridiculous. I cannot be seen to have partisan views on Neighbourhood House.

KEL: Merle's having lunch with her.

BRIAN: Merle. Oh my god. Merle is meeting with my wife. Kel. She'll tell Coral. I know she will. We have to stop them.

KEL: They're down there now.

BRIAN: Kel. You have to help me. You have to go to Neighbourhood House and make sure my wife is never alone with Merle Pickhaver.

KEL: I can't do that.

BRIAN: Why not?

KEL: They don't like me.

BRIAN: Yes they do. Coral likes you. They all like you. And they'll like you even more if you throw in your oar and pretend you want to help them with the campaign.

KEL: But I don't, Brian.

BRIAN: Yes you do Kel. This is one of the most valued community facilities we've got.

KEL: It's a dump.

BRIAN: It's a symbol Kel. A symbol of a community working together in peace and harmony. And to think it could be ripped from our grasp because of mindless worship at the altar of economic rationalism. Kel. You can't let that happen. For the sake of your family, your suburb and the cause of freedom everywhere.

KEL: Oh. All right.

BRIAN: Good man Kel. Good man.

KEL: Brian.

BRIAN: What?

KEL: Just a word of advice.

BRIAN: Yes.

KEL: 'Bout this other business. If I were in your shoes, I'd go tell Coral m'self.

BRIAN: Never. Never, never, never, never!

KEL: Brian. Hear me out. Tell her before anyone else does. Tell her you've been wrong. No. Tell her the truth. You suffered temporary insanity and now you're well, you can't imagine what possessed you to see anything at all in that canniving, manipulative cow –

BRIAN: Kel!

KEL: No. Do it, Brian. And that way, she'll forgive you. Take it from me. I've had experience.

BRIAN: Really?

KEL: Yes. I once had this thing going for a young lass, parking officer. I took the honourable course. Told Betty. Face to face. And we've never looked back. And I knew I'd backed the right horse.

BRIAN: How did you know that Kel? How could you be sure?

KEL: The other lass got hit by a bus.

SCENE EIGHTEEN

The offices of the HON KIMBLE FARKLEY.
FARKLEY *strides forward to shake hands with* DRAGI.

FARKLEY: Mr Smilapski.
DRAGI: Mr Farkley.
FARKLEY: Thank you so much for coming in. I was delighted you called. Delighted. Now what can I get you? Coffee, tea, vodka – [*Aside to* ROCKO] What do Macedonians drink?
ROCKO: Ouzo?
FARKLEY [*aside*]: That's Greek you moron.
DRAGI: A little drop of slivovitz, would be very good.
FARKLEY: Slivovitz. Lovely. Rocko. Slivovitz all round. At eleven o'clock in the morning, why not? Now Mr Smilapski, to what do I owe the pleasure of your visit?
ROCKO: On the rocks, Mr Smilevski?
DRAGI: Neat. And double, please.
FARKLEY: Double. Doubles all round. Why not? On the double. Excuse me for a moment will you.
[FARKLEY *dashes out to consult with* DELORES.]
DRAGI: Is he all right?
ROCKO: Yes. Yes, I think so. Why do you ask?
DRAGI: He seems to be acting like a vlaka.
FARKLEY: Is he Greek or Slavic?
DELORES: Beats me.
FARKLEY: Find out will you.
[FARKLEY *returns.*]
So here's cheers.
[DRAGI *throws it back.* FARKLEY *follows suit.* FARKLEY *splutters.*]
DRAGI: Ah. I think they gave me your glass.
FARKLEY: Sorry?
DRAGI: This is water.

FARKLEY: Rocko. You numbskull. Slivovitz for Mr Smilapski. And one for me too. Cheapskate. Ah, isn't Australia a great country, Mr Slivovitz? Where two men like you and I can talk and drink together and do business as though we both grew up in the same village throwing rocks at donkeys.

DRAGI: I have never thrown a rock at a donkey.

FARKLEY: No. Course you haven't. Neither have I. In fact I've never even seen a donkey. You probably haven't either. What's a donkey?

DRAGI: I've seen many donkeys.

FARKLEY: Yes. Right. Funny old things eh?

DRAGI: What?

FARKLEY: Donkeys.

[*He coughs. Silence.*]

DRAGI: I have a proposal to put to you.

FARKLEY: A proposal. Very good.

DRAGI: I want to start a youth employment scheme.

FARKLEY: Oh my golly, do you.

DRAGI: Yes.

FARKLEY: What an incredibly good idea.

DRAGI: You like it. It's yours.

FARKLEY: This is astonishing. I have been thinking along precisely the same lines. Haven't I Rocko?

ROCKO: Yep. Yessir. You have.

DRAGI: But I'm having trouble with the Council.

FARKLEY: Oh isn't that typical! Bunch of troglodytes eh. Blocking every fresh new initiative. What's their problem this time?

DRAGI: They won't sell me the land.

FARKLEY: The land?

DRAGI: You eat Smilevski Smallgoods?

FARKLEY: Oh absolutely. Smilevski Smallgoods! That's you. Tch! I knew I knew that name. What a numbskull I am.

DRAGI: I want to buy the land next to my factory so I can expand my business. I want Smilevski Smallgoods on every table in the world.

FARKLEY: As you would. I mean don't we all.

DRAGI: I want Greater Burke to be the smallgoods capital of the world.

FARKLEY: Brilliant. Brilliant. I like a man who sees the big picture.
[DELORES *pops her head around the door mouthing "Slavic".*
FARKLEY *doesn't understand. He mouths "What?" She repeats.*]
DRAGI: She says I'm Slavic.
FARKLEY: Oh right. So forgive my ignorance Mr Sinapski, but how does this connect with youth employment.
DRAGI: Oh that. Yes. The Macedonian community –
FARKLEY: Yes. The Macedonian community?
DRAGI: And other small businesses in this electorate want to be involved with a scheme to get young people to work.
FARKLEY: Good. Good. A partnership between Government and small business. I like it. I like it a lot. Initiated from the business community with a strong input from our friends the Macedonians. And backed all the way by this government on the move. And how do you imagine this fantastic scheme working Mr Smilsky?
DRAGI: I thought we'd leave the details for now. Get my people to talk to your people.
FARKLEY: Excellent. Excellent. Big picture. I understand. And I like it.
DRAGI: We just need to discuss two things. The land. Number one. And number two, the media coverage for this event.
FARKLEY: What event is that?
DRAGI: The launch of this scheme at the Town Hall.
FARKLEY: Yes. Yes. We'll have a launch.
DRAGI: I thought we get the Macedonian community to come.
FARKLEY: Yes. Three and half thousand Macedonian small business people in the Town Hall. Yes.
DRAGI: Three and a half thousand. No.
FARKLEY: No?
DRAGI: We'll have seven thousand Macedonians.
FARKLEY: Oh my god. My god. Seven thousand Macedonians. That'll show him. The little prick.
DRAGI: Pardon me.
FARKLEY: Nothing. Nothing at all.
DRAGI: And you will talk to Council.

FARKLEY: I will do more than that Mr Smilevski. I will change the legislation if I have to. Greater Burke will not only be the smallgoods capital of the world. It will be a leader in modern government initiatives. Getting behind the youth of today and giving them a head start for the future. The future Mr Smilevski, is out there and we're going to harness all that youth and vigour and energy to put our small businesses on the map of the world. Yes. Yes. You are a leading light Mr Smilevski. And I feel humbled to have had the priviledge of meeting you. And on the day I will be proud, very proud indeed to stand next to you and shake your hand when we're photographed by every newspaper in the country.

SCENE NINETEEN

Reception.
TREV *and* PIGGY *enter.* TREV *is carrying a cage with a blanket over it.* PIGGY *is noticeably shaken. He is blood stained.*

AMELIA: Piggy! What happened.
TREV: We got him Milly.
[*He barks excitedly.*]
AMELIA: Is that the dog?
TREV: You betcha. Vicious little blighter. Settle. Settle.
AMELIA: Piggy. You look terrible.
TREV: This fella here. [PIGGY] He's a hero. We chased him round and round Smilevski's meat works. Didn't we Pig? Jeez you shoulda seen him go Mil. Sneaky little bugger, this one. I netted him a couple a times, but he wriggled out. Settle! We finally got him out the back o' Neighbourhood House.
PIGGY: He bit a little kid, Mil. And some old codger. Ripped into him.
AMELIA: Oh god. Who was that?
TREV: Dunno. Didn't get a look at him.
PIGGY: There was blood everywhere Mil. It was a battlefield. Everyone was screaming an' yelling. The Serbs were hysterical.

98

Blood and guts from one end of the joint to the other. Snarling and growling. It was a bloody killing field.

TREV: Settle down, Pig. I'll make you a cup of tea.

AMELIA: What happened to the child?

PIGGY: Oh mate. Ambulances and the whole fuckin' lot. It was a killing field, I tell you.

AMELIA: Oh Pig. Come and sit down. What a horrible horrible thing.

TREV: Yeah. Sit down Pig. Take it easy. You were a real hero matey.

[AMELIA *and* TREV *exchange worried glances about* PIGGY*'s emotional state.* AMELIA *leads* PIGGY *off to the lunchroom.*]

I'll just whip to the loo. [*To the cage*] Stay there!

[*The dog is left in reception.* DAWN *walks by. She notices the cage, and peeks under the blanket.*]

DAWN: Kenny! Oh my darling.

[*The dog yaps excitedly. Hearing the flush of the toilet* DAWN *hurries off with the cage to her office.*]

SCENE TWENTY

DAWN*'s office.*

DAWN *puts the cage on her desk. She tries to get him out but it is locked.*

DAWN: Oh Kenny. What have you been up to? Don't tell me you've been a naughty boy. Tsch. Tsch. Tsch. No chokkies for you tonight. Mummy's very cross. See how cross Mummy is? Straight to bed with you. Lights off and no telly.

[*The dog whimpers.*]

Well. That's what happens to naughty boys. Oh all right. You can have a little chokky now, but that's it. No more.

[*Suddenly there's a scream from Reception.*]

AMELIA [*off*]: The dog! Where's the dog?

[*All hell breaks loose.* DAWN *hears yelling and hysterical screaming, doors banging and the sound of people running everywhere. She shoves Kenny in her stationery cupboard*

99

and runs out. DELIA *and* AMELIA *are standing on the desk screaming.*]
AMELIA: Dawn! Dawn! Watch out! There's a dangerous dog. In the Town Hall.
[*People are running everywhere.*]
TREV: Stand back. Stand back. Lock your doors!
[DAWN *rushes into her office. Kenny is barking furiously.*]
DAWN: Ssh. Shutup. Shutup you idiot.
[TREV *bursts in.*]
What's up?
[*She starts to bark to cover for Kenny.*]
TREV: Stand back. He's here. I can hear him.
DAWN: There's no-one here. [*Barks*] He went that way.
TREV: On your desk. Quick.
DAWN: No. He's not here. [*Barking at* TREV]
TREV: That's an order.
[DAWN *clambers on to her desk.*]
Stand back. Settle. He's in there. [*Cupboard*]
[*He gets out his gun and prepares to break down the door.*]
DAWN: No.
[DAWN *jumps down and places herself between the cupboard and* TREV.]
No! Don't hurt him.
[*She throws her arms around his neck and starts kissing him passionately.* TREV *extricates himself and reveals the dog.*]
TREV: Oh my god. Here he is. Oh my god. [*To Kenny*] You sneaky little bugger. Gotta watch you don't I. Turn my back and you're off again. [*To* DAWN] You all right Mrs Snow? Sorry about bein' rude. You know with the order an' everything. You all right?
[*Kenny is jumping up and down excitedly.*]
Look. He likes you.
DAWN: Trev. Trev. You were so brave.
TREV: Just doing a job, missy. Look at him eh? Thinks your Christmas don't he? Eh. Settle down you. Not long for this world poor ol' –
DAWN: What d'you mean? What are you talking about?
TREV: Oh. He's been up to a bit of mischief this fella. Molested a child.
DAWN: No!

TREV: And some ol' bloke. Ripped his arm open.

DAWN: No. I don't believe it.

TREV: 'Fraid so. Very nasty piece of work, this boy when he gets wound up. There'll be a bit o' plastic surgery involved, I'd say. Pity the poor owner.

DAWN: What do you mean?

TREV: Big fines for that kind of damage. I mean someone's gonna have to pick up the tab for that kiddie. And the ol' bloke. Big whack of compo on that one. Yep. And you'll have to be destroyed ol' boy.

> [DAWN *bursts into tears.*]

DAWN: No! You can't. You can't do that.

TREV: Oh. Missy. Please. Don't. Them's the rules. Sorry. Oh. Jeez. I hate this job.

> [TREV *leaves with the cage.* DAWN *sobs inconsolably on her desk.* AMELIA *and* DELIA *enter.*]

AMELIA: Mrs Snow!

> [*She puts her arm around* DAWN.]

Dawn. Oh Dawn. [*To* DELIA] See. She's so sensitive. Dawn, I'm so sorry to have to tell you this. But the man who was savaged by the dog? At Neighbourhood House? It was Kel Carmichael.

> [DAWN *breaks into a new bout of tears.*]

DAWN: Oh poor Kenny.

AMELIA [*gently*]: Kel. Poor Kel. I think she's in shock.

SCENE TWENTY-ONE

The offices of the HON KIMBLE FARKLEY.

FARKLEY [*phone*]: Thank you very much.

> [*He puts down the phone jubilantly.*]

Hot diggety dog! We're in!

> [ROCKO *and* DELORES *whoop for joy.*]

ROCKO: Yes!

FARKLEY: Now Rocko, you get on to the Italians, OK.

ROCKO: Si. Non problemo.

FARKLEY: And Del. You do all the Asian groups. I'll do the Turks.

DELORES: I think my green grocer's a Fijian Indian. Any good?

FARKLEY: Shit yeah. Anyone vaguely ethnic. Round 'em up and rope 'em in.

DELORES: Oh goody.

FARKLEY: Rocko. I got to hand it to you mate. This is an idea made in heaven.

DELORES: The Farkley Global Youth Plan.

ROCKO: I can see history books Sir. Quite frankly.

DELORES: Me too.

FARKLEY: Ten thousand ethnics –

DELORES: All cheering and dancing, spilling out of the Town Hall, onto the streets.

ROCKO: And there you'll be Sir. The man of the moment.

DELORES: The man of the people.

ROCKO: The Henry Kissinger of Greater Burke. The Greeks'll be shaking hands with the Turks, embracing the Macos. The Serbs dancing with the Croats. The Tamil Tigers –

DELORES: – Muslim separatists –

ROCKO: – The Taleban Islamic Militia Brass Band.

DELORES: If we can get them.

ROCKO: We'll get them Del. This is one gig a band like that'd kill to be at.

FARKLEY: Yeah. And you know what's so beautiful? To think that only a couple of thousand turned up when that little prick opened the Macedonian Church.

DELORES: Yeah. They stayed at home in droves. Says a lot for his popularity I reckon.

ROCKO: He's just not in touch with the grass roots. That's all there is to it. You know, Kimble, Sir, we could even be looking at a leadership spill over this one.

FARKLEY: Ah ha. Rocko you're a mind reader.

ROCKO: One of my many talents, Sir
    [*The phone rings.*]

DELORES: Good morning. Offices of Kimble Farkley. Hello. Yes. Yes. Of course. Just one moment please. [*To* FARKLEY] It's the Premier.

FARKLEY: Mr Premier. How are you Sir. Jolly good. Lunch? Ho! Not to worry. I understand these things. Yes, Yes of course. The Macedonians – Pushy? Oh I wouldn't say that Sir. I enjoy very good relations with the Macedonians. In fact one of my best friends is a Macedonian. Dinner. Why not? Jolly good. I'll just get my diary. [*To* DELORES] Del, quick, what's the date of the Town Hall launch?

DELORES: The twenty-third.

FARKLEY [*phone*]: What about the twenty-third? Somewhere over your side of town. Excellent. See you then.

    [*Hangs up.*]

    Ha! That'll fix you, you miserable bastard!

SCENE TWENTY-TWO

Offices of the Dog Catcher.
PIGGY *and* TREV *sit alone in their office with Kenny in his cage on the table.* TREV *eats a sandwich feeding his crusts through the bars to Kenny.*

TREV: You've got one last request Ken. Anything you like? Just name it.

PIGGY: How come you call him Ken?

TREV: It's on his tag. Come on Ken. You can tell me. Your last wish, spit it out.

    [*He leans in close.*]

    Oh, dunno about that.

    [*Pause.*]

    He wants to be let out.

PIGGY: Get real.

TREV: He wants another chance, Pig. We all make mistakes.

PIGGY: No way.

TREV: He says he'll do a hundred hours of community service.

PIGGY: Die, you mongrel.

    [*Kenny snaps viciously.* PIGGY *jumps back from the cage.*]

TREV: Now Pig, that is no way to treat a dog.

PIGGY: That is not a dog. That is a murderer.

TREV: Pig, can I tell you something?

PIGGY: What?

TREV: Scout's honour you won't tell?

PIGGY: No way. I hate those fuckin' scouts. I had to go to this barbie once at Kel's house. Worst day of my fuckin' life.

TREV: OK. Just say you won't tell and I'll trust you.

PIGGY: Yeah. Come on.

TREV: You gotta say.

PIGGY: Oh Christ. I promise I will not tell, and if I do, so help me God, I'll kiss Dawn Snow's bum.

[TREV's *hand inadvertently reaches up and wipes his mouth, removing a memory of the kiss.*]

TREV: OK. That should do it. You know how we keep dogs in the pound and after twenty-eight days if no-one comes to claim 'em, we dispose of them?

PIGGY: Yeah.

TREV: I never done it.

PIGGY: What?

TREV: I let 'em go.

PIGGY: You don't.

TREV: I make sure they have a big feed up, give 'em five bucks and send 'em on their way.

PIGGY: You give them five dollars.

TREV: Just a lend. Mostly I get it back. See, nine times out of ten, I have to catch 'em again.

PIGGY: You're off your nut.

TREV: I can't do it Pig. I can't kill a dog.

PIGGY: But what happens if it's a dangerous dog.

TREV: Yeah. I hate it when that happens. But if I ruly ruly have to destroy it, then I ... um ... well I subcontract the work.

PIGGY: Trev, you know something. You're a mental case.

TREV: Pig. I'm gonna tell you a little statistic. We get more dogs through our books than any other Dog Catcher department in this state.

PIGGY: That's because you keep letting 'em out and catching 'em again.

104

TREV: Yeah. Little bit of a rotation system happening. I admit. But because of the very heavy demands on this department, we had to put another bloke on, didn't we. See.

PIGGY: Oh. So I should be thankful.

TREV: Yeah. That did occur to me Pig.

PIGGY: You know what this reminds me of?

TREV: What?

PIGGY: The voting at last Council election.

SCENE TWENTY-THREE

Corridor outside the Dog Catcher's offices.
The two SMILEVSKI BOYS *stride down the corridor as though they are Joe Pesci and Robert de Niro in a Scorscesi movie.*

LADE: OK we're gonna fuckin' do it. We're gonna take this mother fucker out. Fuck it.

MILE: Yeah. Fuck it.
    [*They kick the door open and stand with guns poised.* TREV *and* PIGGY *jump up to their feet.*]
    OK. Where's this dude?

LADE: Where is he?
    [TREV *points at Kenny. The dog whimpers.*]

MILE: That is a dog.

LADE: You said a contract on some fuckin' dude called Kenny.

TREV: I said a dog. A dog called Kenny.

MILE: That is one dangerous mother fucker. Stand back.
    [*They raise their guns to shoot.*]

TREV: Stop!

LADE: What?

TREV: Look. I just can't go through with this today. Um. Maybe tomorrow.

MILE: What?

TREV: Just another twenty-four hours OK. I'll call you. Thanks.

MILE: Tomorrow?

TREV: Yeah.

LADE: That is one weird dude.

105

SCENE TWENTY-FOUR

Reception.
Morning. KEL *arrives at work. He is completely bandaged up except for two eye holes. The other staff are loitering in Reception.*

AMELIA: Kel! Is that you?
    [KEL *nods.*]
KEL: I thought I better make a bit of an effort. Come into work. Despite the pain.
DELIA: You got some envelopes there Amelia? In the drawer?
KEL: The pain is almost unendurable you know.
DELIA: No. The long ones.
KEL: I think I understand the true meaning of the word "agony".
AMELIA: These?
DELIA: Haven't you got any plain ones?
AMELIA: Nup.
    [KEL *starts to groan piteously and loudly.*]
    There'll be some in the stationery cupboard.
DELIA: Righteo.
KEL: So how are you today Delia? Good?
DELIA: Amelia, could you tell him I don't talk to scabs.
    [*She walks off.*]
AMELIA: Are you intending to book people today?
KEL: Some of us have got quotas to work to Amelia.
AMELIA: You don't look a well man Kel.
KEL: I was attacked by a dog.
AMELIA: Yeah.
    [*She busies herself with her work.*]
KEL: Where's Brian?
AMELIA: He's here somewhere. He was attacked by his wife.
    [BRIAN *comes out of his office. He is in similar circumstances: head bandaged, arm in a sling etc.*]
KEL: Brian!

[BRIAN *gives* AMELIA *a document.*]

BRIAN: Thanks a lot Kel. Next time I want some advice, I'll know you're the very person to avoid.

[*He walks back into his office and shuts the door.*]

SCENE TWENTY-FIVE

BRIAN'*s office.*

BRIAN *and* KEL. BRIAN *has a large suitcase open on his desk with all his belongings. There is a camp bed, laid out next to the desk.*

BRIAN: Here. Give me a hand with this.

[*The two walking wounded attempt to pack up the bed.*]

KEL: So, what happened?

BRIAN: Well I decided to take your advice and tell Coral. And now I am living in my office. That's about it really.

KEL: You should have gone to Dawn's. I mean if Coral is going to behave like that –

BRIAN: – I did. I went to Dawn's.

KEL: And?

BRIAN: She was entertaining someone else.

KEL: What a bitch! Here. What do I do with your jarmies?

[BRIAN *snatches them.*]

BRIAN: And you know who that someone else was?

KEL: Who?

BRIAN: Trevor.

KEL: Your brother?

BRIAN: Mmm.

KEL: That two timing bitch!

[*There is a knock at the door.* TREVOR *enters.*]

Trevor. I am surprised you dare show your face around here.

[TREV *looks confusedly from one bandaged head to the other.*]

BRIAN: What were you doing at Dawn Snow's house last night Trevor. At approximately 10.20pm?

TREV: Ten twenty?

107

BRIAN: Approximately.

TREV: Um. We were talking.

KEL: Oh I've heard that before. We were just talking, your honour! Pull the other one Trev.

TREV: We were talking about the Dog Show. Mrs Snow is going to judge the clipping and grooming section.

KEL: Is that so? Clipping and grooming.

TREV: I asked Merle Pickhaver, but she scrunched it up and threw it out the window.

[*Pause.*]

What's all this?

BRIAN: These are all my worldly possessions, Trev. What you see is all I have.

TREV: Did you sleep here?

BRIAN: Yes. This is where I live now.

TREV: Really. Coral doesn't mind?

BRIAN: Apparently not.

TREV: S'ppose it cuts down travelling time.

BRIAN: Mm. It's very convenient, that way.

TREV: Oh well.

KEL: I trust that you've dealt with the dog, Trevor.

TREV: What dog? Oh. That dog.

KEL: Yes. That dog.

BRIAN: Actually that was one thing about last night. This would have been quite comfortable, in its own unhappy little way, except I was kept awake by some bloody dog barking. Sounded like it was coming from the basement.

TREV: Excuse me for a tick. I have to go.

[TREV *exits hastily.*]

TWENTY-SIX

The corridor outside BRIAN's *office.*

TREV *is accosted by* DAWN *and dragged into her office.*

DAWN: Trevor! Just the man.

[DAWN *closes the door and leads him by the hand to a seat.*]
Trevor. Trevor. You look tense. Let me give your shoulders a bit of a rub.
[TREV *looks deeply uncomfortable.*]
I'm so glad you came over last night.
TREV: Ow.
DAWN: Too hard?
TREV: Arggh.
DAWN: You are tense. Goodness me. I'm just getting into some shiatsu points here.
TREV: Yow.
[*He leaps up.*]
DAWN: Actually Trev, there's a bit of an unpleasant smell in here. Can you smell anything?
TREV: Nope.
DAWN: Smells like –
TREV: Cat's piss?
DAWN: Mmm.
TREV: Yeah. Probl'y me.
DAWN: Right.
[*She moves away, smelling her fingers.*]
Trev. I had this idea.
TREV: Is this about the dog?
DAWN: Yes. How did you guess? You haven't done anything ... awful, have you?
TREV: No. Not yet.
DAWN: I thought you and I could have a little secret.
TREV: What sort of a secret?
DAWN: I thought you could give that poor little misunderstood dog to me.
TREV: No can do. Sorry.
DAWN: But I've got a back yard Trev. He'd never get out.
TREV: Nope.
DAWN: Please?
TREV: Nup.
[DAWN *gives a pleading little bark with her hands in a dog begging position.* TREV *woofs back indicating the negative.* DAWN *whines.* TREV *ruffs – definitely not.*]

Ruff. Nup. Ruff. Nup.

DAWN: Trevor! I cannot abide sadism. And that's what this is. It's brutality. And I cannot, in all conscience stand by and let this take place under my nose.

TREV: I wouldn't do it in here M'am.

DAWN: You won't do it at all. You are going to get that dog –

TREV: The dog's gone M'am.

DAWN: Where's the dog gone?

> [TREVOR *points down.*]
> In the ground?

TREV: Sort of –

DAWN: Dead?

TREV: M'am. I'll lose m' job.

> [DAWN *rushes at him and tries to strangle him.*]

DAWN: Is the dog dead? Tell me!!

> [*She is shaking his head back and forth.*]

TREV: No. M'am. Listen. I understand how opposed you are to any sort of violence but if I don't dispose of that dog I'll get it in the neck.

DAWN: Trevor, can I tell you something. In my desk here I have an inventory of seventy-five items that have been stolen from this Town Hall in the past six months. Now I happen to know you are involved in this up to your neck.

TREV: No.

DAWN: Wait. Now if I am asked to weigh up which of the two crimes – theft on the one hand, or cold blooded murder on the other – If I am asked to say which I find the most reprehensible, I would have to say the premeditated murder of an innocent. Give me the dog Trevor. Give me the dog, or I will be forced to hand you over to the police.

> [*There is a knock at the door,* AMELIA *enters.*]

AMELIA: Excuse me, Dawn. Mr Farkley's here.

DAWN: Oh.

AMELIA: The meeting's in The Mayoral Suite.

DAWN: Thank you Amelia.

> [AMELIA *exits.* DAWN *grabs her coat.*]
> We're talking about a jail sentence Trevor. Years and years in a damp cold cell, all alone. And who'll look after your dog? He'll

just be left to die in your flat. No food. No water. Think about that. I'd say five years minimum. And this time, no one, not even Brian'd put in a good word for you.

SCENE TWENTY-SEVEN

The Mayoral Suite.
DAWN, FARKLEY, DRAGI, MERLE *and* BRIAN *are in a meeting.*
AMELIA *wheels in a trolley of beverages and cakes.*

DAWN: Thank you Amelia.
    [DAWN *helps herself to a cake.*]
FARKLEY: Mrs Snow.
DAWN [*mouthful*]: Mmm.
FARKLEY: What would you say our greatest asset is?
DAWN: Mmm.
AMELIA: Mr Farkley?
    [*She hands him a cup of tea.*]
FARKLEY: Thank you.
BRIAN: I think she would say it's Neighbourhood House.
FARKLEY: Mrs Snow?
DAWN: Mmm.
FARKLEY: You don't agree Mrs Pickhaver.
MERLE: Oh I do. I think Neighbourhood House is one of this community's major assets. But possibly not for the same reason Mrs Snow would regard it as an asset.
FARKLEY: Mm. Well I'd have to disagree with both of you I'm afraid. As I think Mr Smilevski would.
DRAGI: I would?
FARKLEY: I think Mr Smilevski and I are both in agreement on this one. I think we would say that this community's greatest asset was our youth. And we have twenty-five thousand young people in this electorate.
MERLE: Twenty thousand of whom are unemployed.
FARKLEY: Yes. They are. It is a statistic which grieves me, more than I can express. As it does Mr Smilevski.

111

DRAGI: Yes. It causes me big grief. Terrible.

MERLE: May I just ask – forgive me – but what is Mr Smilevski doing at this meeting?

FARKLEY: Mr Smilevski is here because as President of The Chamber of Commerce –

MERLE: You're not President of –

DRAGI: I was.

FARKLEY: He was. He was indeed. And during his time as President a great many reforms took place in the business community, from which we have all benefitted, significantly.

MERLE: Name one.

DAWN: Excuse me.

FARKLEY: Sorry?

DAWN: Could you pass those er – ?

FARKLEY: Sandwiches?

DAWN: No. Er, the little pastry thingos.

FARKLEY: These?

DAWN: Thank you.

FARKLEY: He is also of course a very eminent member of the Macedonian community, in touch with the needs and aspirations of one of our largest and most exciting ethnic groups. Because of this I sought out Mr Smilevski to put to him a little idea of mine that's been knocking around for some time. And naturally being a man of immense humanity and vision, he has come to the party with enormous enthusiasm.

MERLE: So what's the idea?

DRAGI: You sell me Neighbourhood House.

MERLE: Don't be ridiculous. Council wouldn't consider that in a million years.

FARKLEY: Mrs Pickhaver. Let me step in. Personally I think Neighbourhood House is an exceptional community facility. And I know Mr Smilevski would concur wholeheartedly.

DRAGI: Yes. I do. It's a dump.

DAWN: Dragi.

[*She pops a cake in his mouth.*]

Why don't you let Mr Farkley do the talking for a bit.

FARKLEY: Yes. I feel Neighbourhood House is a shining example of multicultural unity. And I think it's an achievement of which,

112

you especially, should be duly proud. But what I need to do and what I want to do, is extend that concept further. I want to involve every ethnic group in this city to work together to give our young people a chance. I have two daughters Mrs Pickhaver and I grieve for them. Life for them is not like it was for you and I. Our youth was a time for experimentation, optimism, Stop the Vietnam War, have a go, drop out, give it a try, see if it works. And that was because we always knew Mrs Pickhaver that there was a job for us, when we were ready to drop back in. Our young people now don't have that luxury. And all I am trying to do with Mr Smilevski's help – and countless other business people – is to give young people some hope. Now I don't doubt for a minute that Neighbourhood House isn't fulfilling that niche in a small way. But we need to invest in a bigger scheme. Not just for leisure activities, but for work. For a sense of real purpose which is going to bind our community in terms of committment and collaboration to a shared ideal.

And I think sometimes, very good things have to be sacrificed to make way for great things.

[*Silence.* AMELIA *claps. Everyone, except* MERLE, *joins in.*]

SCENE TWENTY-EIGHT

Town Hall basement.
A single globe dangles from the roof creating a bunker effect. This is the place where DELIA *and* MERLE *have chosen to conduct their secret meetings to Save The House.* MERLE, DELIA *and* PIGGY *enter with a torch and then switch the light on.*

DELIA: What d'you reckon?
    [*They survey the place.*]
MERLE: It's a bit cold.
DELIA: No one would ever find us here.
PIGGY: That's for sure.
DELIA: Look.
    [*She unfurls a banner: "Save The House".*]

MERLE: Well I suppose it's as good as anywhere for campaign headquarters.

DELIA: Barry said he'd rig up phones and faxes and stuff.

MERLE: Great.

[*She picks up the phone on the desk.*]

It works.

DELIA: So tell us what happened at the meeting with Farkley.

MERLE: He's got this idea for a youth employment scheme.

DELIA: Oh yeah.

MERLE: He's going to have a big launch at the Town Hall and he wants me to be a speaker.

DELIA: What? I thought he hated you.

MERLE: He does. He loathes me. And I loathe him.

PIGGY: That's good.

MERLE: But we pretend we're terribly friendly and we're both on the same side.

DELIA: So what's the deal? What's he want?

MERLE: Farkley wants me to lobby the other councillors to sell Neighbourhood House.

DELIA: You're joking.

MERLE: And you know who's behind all this?

DELIA: Who? Dawn Snow?

MERLE: Dragi Smilevski.

DELIA: You're kidding.

MERLE: Nope. Smilevski's behind the whole thing. In terms of Neighbourhood House, he's Public Enemy Number One.

PIGGY: I'll tell you something about the Smilevski's. They're moonlighting for Trev.

MERLE: What?

PIGGY: Trev subcontracts the work at the pound. He gets the Smilevski's to dispose of dangerous dogs.

MERLE: Christ! They're into everything. Smilevski senior wants to make Greater Burke the smallgoods capital of Australia.

DELIA: That's probably what they do with the dogs. Put 'em in the salami.

MERLE: Oh Delia!

PIGGY: Are you thinking what I'm thinking?

DELIA: I dunno. What are you thinking?

PIGGY: I'm thinking, what *do* they do with those dogs? I mean a little meat substitution racket. It's happened before.
MERLE: Piggy.
PIGGY: That's pretty heavy shit.
DELIA: It's disgusting.
PIGGY: I mean it's enough to close a business down.
DELIA: If it got out.
PIGGY: Yeah.
MERLE: Stop it, you two.
PIGGY: I mean, would you eat that salami?
DELIA: I still don't eat peanut butter.
PIGGY: Merle. I'm not saying this is going on. I'm not. But this is a public health issue. And the public have a right to know what's actually in the salami.
DELIA: I agree with Piggy. I think it's in the public interest.
PIGGY: I think we have a moral responsibility actually.
DELIA: Me too.
MERLE: Are you sure the Smilevski's are involved with this?
PIGGY: I saw it with my own two eyes.
[*Suddenly there is a noise. The sound of a door opening.*]
MERLE: What's that?
PIGGY: Someone's there.
DELIA: Quick!
[*They hit the lights and hide under the desk. In the darkness, a figure stumbles about. We hear a male voice, "Ken?" "Kenny?" "You there boy?"* TREV *turns the light on.*]
TREV: Ken? Kenny?
[*We hear barking coming from a side room.* TREV *exits and returns with a very excited Kenny on a leash, jumping and barking. Kenny tries to pull* TREV *over to the desk but he keeps reigning him in.*]
Where are you off to, you silly bugger. Ssh. Keep it down. Come on, you and me are going for a walk.
[TREV *is about to lead Kenny away when* BRIAN *appears around the corner in his pyjamas, carrying a lantern. Both men leap in fright. The dog barks wildly.*]
BRIAN: What is *that* doing here?
TREV: Um, I was just ... um ... taking him for a walk.

115

BRIAN: Whose dog is that Trevor?

TREV: Um. It's Mrs Snow's. It's her dog. I was just taking him ... um ... back.

BRIAN: Is that the dog that savaged Kel Carmichael?

TREV: No. No it is not. That's another dog. And that dog's been destroyed.

BRIAN: Are you lying to me Trevor?

TREV: No.

BRIAN: Well why is your left nostril twitching?

TREV: Um ...

BRIAN: Well we can solve this very quickly, can't we?

[*He picks up the phone on the desk, and dials a number.*]

Dawn. It's Brian. Don't hang up! Dawn, do you owe a pit bull terrier that answers to the name of –

TREV: Kenny.

BRIAN: Kenny?

[*Pause.*]

Thank you Dawn. Good night. Well that solves it doesn't it Trevor. Mrs Snow does not own a pit bull terrier by the name of Kenny. In fact she can't understand why anyone would keep a pet that had the capacity to savage innocent children and parking officers.

TREV: Brian, she's going to put me in jail.

BRIAN: If she doesn't, I will.

[BRIAN *exits.* PIGGY *jumps up from behind the desk.* TREV *nearly jumps out of his skin.*]

PIGGY: Give me the dog Trev.

[BRIAN *re-enters.* PIGGY *dives back under the desk.*]

BRIAN: And another thing. If that dog is not dead by tomorrow morning, I'll be looking for another Dog Catcher.

[BRIAN *exits.*]

PIGGY: You heard the man Trev. Give me the dog. Come on. I'll take it down to Smilevski's.

TREV: I can't.

PIGGY: Your job's on the line, buddy.

[MERLE *and* DELIA *emerge.*]

TREV: Cripes. What is this?

DELIA: Give him the dog Trev.

TREV: She knows about the furniture and stuff. She's gonna put me in jail.

DELIA: What?

TREV: The fat lady. She knows we've been nicking computers and stuff.

DELIA: Shit.

MERLE: Amelia.

TREV: She says unless I give her the dog, she'll turn me over to the cops.

MERLE: Why does she want the dog?

DELIA: Because that's her dog. Must be.

[*She starts to laugh hysterically. The dog barks. She jumps back.*]

Hey Trev. Can you keep that thing reigned in. That is Dawn Snow's dog.

TREV: I made that up. It's not her dog.

MERLE: She said it wasn't her dog.

DELIA: 'Course it's her dog. You idiots! She's not gonna own up that it's her dog.

MERLE: Whose dog is it Trev?

TREV: I dunno.

MERLE: Haven't you got records?

TREV: Um. There's a bit of a back log up there. With the registrations. It's not on the computer.

PIGGY: She knows about the stuff. That's a bit of a worry.

DELIA: But we know about the dog. Let's just work this out. Whatever we do, we can't get rid of the dog. Not yet. [*To Kenny*] We need you, you repulsive creature.

[*Kenny snarls.*]

Trev!

TREV: Don't worry. I got him.

DELIA: Merle?

MERLE: Don't look at me. I hate dogs.

[*Kenny snarls.*]

Present company excepted.

DELIA: What about Brian's place?

TREV: Oh sure.

DELIA: Well he's not there. He's upstairs.

MERLE: And Coral's staying at her sister's.
DELIA: That's it.We'll take it to Brian's. And we need to get rid of all the stuff at Neighbourhood House. It's too risky.
PIGGY: Maybe we could put that at Brian's too.
TREV: In the shed out the back.
DELIA: Perfect! Come on. Let's get out of here.

SCENE TWENTY-NINE

DAWN SNOW's office.
DAWN is meeting with AMELIA.

DAWN: Look, this is the way I figure it. There are twelve Councillors. These five are for the sale and these six are against it.
AMELIA: Five and six are eleven. Who's the twelth?
DAWN: Brian. He's the wild card.
AMELIA: Yeah, but even if Brian votes for the sale, that'll make it a tie.
DAWN: I know. We need to secure Brian's vote and somehow get one of these idiots to change their mind.
AMELIA: Before six thirty tonight.
DAWN: Yeah.
AMELIA: Well who is there? Evans. Cotterill. Vladic.
DAWN: No. Forget it. I've tried. Merle Pickhaver's got them round her little finger.
    [Pause.]
    I think I might be able to work on Brian, but as for the others – ?
AMELIA: What would happen if someone didn't turn up. Someone who was against the sale. Someone like Merle Pickhaver.
DAWN: If it was Merle Pickhaver, we'd have to defer the decision. And we can't afford to do that.
AMELIA: But what if something terrible happened.
DAWN: Like what?
AMELIA: I dunno. A car accident or something.

DAWN: Amelia! Anyway knowing Pickhaver even if she was in an iron lung, she'd still turn up.
[*There is a knock at the door and* KEL *pops his bandaged head around the door.*]
KEL: Sorry Mrs S. Sorry to interrupt. I wonder if you could pop your signature on this.
DAWN: Righteo. There you are.
KEL: Thank you very much. Amelia.
AMELIA: Kel.
[KEL *exits.*]
DAWN: That's it. I've got it. You're a genius, Milly.
AMELIA: What? What did I say?
DAWN: You've just convinced me. Merle Pickhaver will be there tonight. At the Council meeting. But surprise. Surprise. Do you know, she's going to vote for the sale of Neighbourhood House.

SCENE THIRTY

BRIAN'*s office*
DAWN *knocks and enters. Coquettishly she slips the lock on his door.*

DAWN: Brian. Bri, Bri.
BRIAN: Dawn!
DAWN: Look at you, all holed up here in your lonesome little office. Tsch. I'm worried about you.
BRIAN: Dawn. I.. er.
DAWN: I don't know why you haven't come to visit little ol' me. I've been so lonesome.
BRIAN: I did Dawn. If you remember. But you were obviously seeing someone else.
DAWN: Now you know that's not true. Are these yours?
[*She holds up his pyjamas. He snatches them off her. She snatches them back.*]
If I can't have you, then at least let me have these.
BRIAN: I can't do that Dawn.

DAWN: Why not?

BRIAN: Because I don't have anything else to sleep in. And it gets very cold in here.

DAWN: Oh I bet it does. Cold and lonely. Brian. This is not right. A man like you, all alone. What happened to us Brian? What happened to the most romantic summer of our lives? Do you remember the first time you kissed me?

BRIAN: Um No. When was that. Remind me.

DAWN: You were showing me around Waste Disposal.

BRIAN: Oh yes.

DAWN: That was the sweetest kiss I've ever had. A stolen kiss. A kiss that promised things: excitement, thrill, sensual delirium.

BRIAN: Oh Dawn.

DAWN: I was faint with happiness. And I spent every waking hour, longing, yearning, aching. I'd give anything Brian. Anything at all to have that back.

BRIAN: Oh Dawn.

[He moves to embrace her.]

DAWN: But! Of course it can't be. That's the tragedy Brian. That is the anguish and the misery of this god forsaken life, that is mine. A love that can never be.

BRIAN: But why Dawn? Why not?

DAWN: Oh Brian. I would ask you to come to me tonight, if it were not for one little thing that's stopping us. One little problem.

BRIAN: Coral?

DAWN: No. Not Coral. Coral's never been a problem.

BRIAN: Well what then Dawn? Tell me.

DAWN: It's just a sexual thing.

BRIAN: A sexual thing? You've never complained before.

DAWN: That's because it's never been a problem before.

BRIAN: Well I can't imagine what it could be, Dawn. Frankly, I have never had any problems in that department.

DAWN: I know darling. It's not you. It's me. And this is very hard for me to tell you, but ... I do find it hard to get aroused when the man who I'm in bed with, is .... irresponsible.

BRIAN: But Dawn. That's not true. I'm always responsible. I always –

DAWN: Not always.

120

BRIAN: Well once. Once. But you said you didn't mind.

DAWN: I'm talking about fiscal responsibility. Brian. I'm talking about a 4.8 million dollar shortfall. It's come between us Brian and it won't go away.

BRIAN: Oh Dawn.

DAWN: I'm sorry but it's a big turn off. I can't help it. And you just seem to act as if that sort of thing is a woman's responsibility.

BRIAN: I'm sorry Dawn. I didn't realise. If only you knew how much I adore you. I worship you Dawn.

DAWN: But not that much.

[*Silence.*]

Of course there are things you could do. If you wanted to. If you really wanted to make love to me again. As I do Brian. I want to feel as I felt before.

BRIAN: I want you to Dawn.

DAWN: I want me to, too.

BRIAN: Oh Dawn that makes both of us.

DAWN: I want you to put your hand up tonight Brian. I want you to say yes. Yes. Yes.

BRIAN: Yes.

DAWN: Yes to the sale of Neighbourhood House. But what you're really saying is yes. Yes. I want to sexually liberate the woman I love.

BRIAN: Yes.

[*They fall in to a passionate embrace.*]

SCENE THIRTY-ONE

Reception.
MERLE *approaches* AMELIA.

MERLE: Evening Milly. Everything all set for the meeting.

AMELIA: Oh Merle. Hi. I'm so glad you're early. Mrs Snow has some news about Neighbourhood House.

MERLE: What sort of news.

AMELIA: Good news.

121

MERLE: What is good news for her is not good news for me.

AMELIA: Ooh. I think you might be surprised.

[*Pause.*]

Go on in. She's waiting to see you.

[MERLE *crosses the floor and knocks on* DAWN's *door. She enters.*]

SCENE THIRTY-TWO

MERLE *looks around to find* MRS SNOW's *room empty.*

MERLE: Mrs Snow? Mrs Snow?

[*She hears noises coming from the cupboard. She opens the door and looks in.* DAWN *jumps out the other side and pushes her in, locking the door.*]

DAWN: Not that ol' trick again. You fall for it, every time don't you Merle.

[DAWN *rushes out to signal to* AMELIA *to come in.* BRIAN *sweeps through Reception.*]

BRIAN: Ah Mrs Snow. Ready for the meeting.

DAWN [*purposefully*]: Yes. What about you?

BRIAN: Yes. Yes. Yes.

[DAWN *steals a risque kiss, in a public place.*]

DAWN: But Brian. Have you heard the news?

BRIAN: No. What?

DAWN: Poor Merle. She's so brave.

BRIAN: What?

DAWN: After all she's been through, she is still going to come. My respect for that woman knows no bounds. After today.

Council Chambers.

CLERK: Ladies and gentlemen. Would you all rise.

[*The Mayor and all the Councillors file into the space.* BRIAN *takes his place in the Mayoral Chair.* DAWN *enters last pushing an unrecognisable* AMELIA, *bandaged from head to foot, in a wheelchair with a drip.*]

BRIAN: Make way for Mrs Pickhaver please. Thank you Dawn. [*Addressing the Councillors and gallery*] Ladies and gentleman, it is my melancholy duty to inform you that one of our Councillors, representing the East Ward, Mrs Merle Pickhaver, was last night in a terrible accident. But with the indomitable spirit which we have come to know and love, Mrs Pickhaver has made the supreme sacrifice and is here with us tonight. Ladies and gentlemen, Mrs Merle Pickhaver.

[*The gallery applaud.* MERLE *raises a courageous hand to wave to the crowd.*]

Thank you. Please be seated. Ladies and gentlemen we have a very, very long agenda tonight so I would ask for your patience and your keen attention.

[DAWN *whispers to* BRIAN *who nods gravely.*]

Under the circumstances, considering Mrs Pickhaver's delicate condition it would seem wise to move Agenda Item Number 43, forward. So the new order will be minutes from last Council meeting on 12th of the 8th, apologies, business arising and the CEO's report. We will then move straight to Item 43, which we will call Item Number Five.

[MERLE *starts to groan.* BRIAN *looks over to* DAWN, *who is shaking her head compassionately.*]

DAWN: Mayor Guest With the indulgence of Council, I would request that we move directly to Agenda Item 43. We may not be able to expect Councillor Pickhaver to last the distance.

BRIAN: Right. Item Number 43. Page 600, Ladies and gentleman. The Sale of Neighbourhood House.

This issue has been canvassed very thoroughly at our last meeting and I draw your attention to the minutes of that discussion. Pages 112 to 345. I trust you have all availed yourself of the opportunity to read and consider all the arguments.

[*General mumbling from the floor.*]

Could I have a show of hands please. All those against the sale of Neighbourhood House. Raise your hands please.

[*He counts.*]

Five. All those in favour.

[*He counts five. Slowly, painfully,* MERLE *raises her plastered leg.*]

Is that a "yes".

DAWN: Yes.

[*Pause.*]

Brian, you haven't voted.

[BRIAN *raises his hand, staring ardently at* DAWN.]

BRIAN: Yes!

DAWN: Yes! That makes seven.

CLERK: Seven ayes, five nays. Ladies and gentlemen, the ayes have it. Council has decided that Neighbourhood House will be sold.

[*The gallery errupts with boos and hisses.*]

SCENE THIRTY-FOUR

Next morning. TREV *ambles through Reception whistling. He knocks and enters* DAWN SNOW'*s office. After a few minutes* TREV *is ejected backwards out the door.* MERLE PICKHAVER *comes flying past him.*

MERLE [*yelling*]: Get out of my way!

[*She exits through the back doors.*]

AMELIA: Who was that?

TREV: Merle Pickhaver, I think. Cripes.

AMELIA: Cripes.

TREV: You know something Mil. That is the second time I've found Merle Pickhaver hiding in Dawn Snow's stationery cupboard. What d'you make of that?

AMELIA: Gee Trev. I dunno.

TREV: You don't think it's a bit kinky do you?

AMELIA: A bit kinky? I think it's very kinky.

TREV: That's what I reckon. Kinky.

AMELIA: Still, she hasn't been the same since her accident.

TREV: That's what Brian said. He said – [*Leaning forward whispering*] – "Head injuries".

[AMELIA *nods gravely.*]

SCENE THIRTY-FIVE

The offices of the HON KIMBLE FARKLEY.

FARKLEY: Mr Smilevski. Congratulations. My goodness me. Well done.

DRAGI: Thank you. Thank you. We signed the deal last night. After the Council meeting.

FARKLEY: And I believe Mrs Pickhaver came to the party. My goodness me. How the worm turns.

DRAGI: Mr Farkley, I have to say, you are not just a politician. You are a statesman. A man of integrity and great humanity. I was moved by your speech and so too was The Pickhaver. Who could not have been? Sir, I feel humbled to have had the privilege of doing business. And on the day I will be proud, very proud indeed to stand next to you and shake your hand when we're photographed by every newspaper in the country.

[*He embraces* FARKLEY.]

FARKLEY: Mr Smilevski. I can't tell you how much that means to me, coming from you. Slivovitz?

DRAGI: Ah! Why not!

[*They clink glasses.*]

To youth!

FARKLEY: And smallgoods!

SCENE THIRTY-SIX

The Town Hall basement.
DELIA, PIGGY *and* MERLE *are dressed in army fatigues.*

MERLE: Delia. Piggy. You and I have always played by the rules. We have always acted with integrity and great humanity. We have worked within the system because of an unshakeable belief that democracy and justice would always triumph. But, my friends, last night my faith was shattered. Piggy. Delia. The terrible truth is that there are no longer rules. We find ourselves at the end of this millenium living and working in a facist dictatorship and there is no other option but to choose ... terrorism.
PIGGY: Yae!!!

SCENE THIRTY-SEVEN

The Town Hall.
It is the night of the launch. The stage is decked with the banner –
The Farkley Global Youth Plan. The stage is festooned with little
flags from every country in the world. "Smilevskis is Smarvellous"
banners adorn the walls. PIGGY's *enthusiastic Yae!! is taken up by*
the roar of the CROWD *as* BRIAN *in mayoral robes,* FARKLEY, DAWN
and DRAGI *walk in procession up onto the stage. "Advance*
Australia Fair" blares through the loud speakers. (The audience
are urged to stand to join in the national anthem with the words
projected overhead.) BRIAN *takes the microphone.*

BRIAN: Ladies and gentlemen, as Mayor of Greater Burke and a citizen of this great country of ours, it gives me enormous pleasure to welcome you all here tonight, which must be one of

126

the greatest celebrations this suburb has ever seen. Ladies and gentlemen, of every race, creed, ethnic origin, religious and political belief, tonight is our time to join together –

[*Suddenly on a false cue the Macedonian folkloric dancers burst onto the stage and do their number.*]

Ladies and gentlemen, The Macedonian Folkloric dancers!

[*As they file out in a dancing procession we see an awkward* TREV, *attempting to stage manage and getting dragged into their midst. He is handed a kerfchief and has to try to follow the dance steps.*]

Thank you. Thank you. The Macedonian Folkloric dancers. Ladies and Gentlemen. Give them a big hand.

[SMILEVSKI *passes* BRIAN *a note.*]

Mr Smilevski has just asked me to tell you that the catering tonight is courtesy of Smilevskis is Smarvellous Smallgoods. So please avail yourselves of the sausage sizzles at the various points around the Town Hall. At very reduced rates. Moreover the good ladies from the Little Sisters of the Needy will be handing around platters of salami sandwiches. Please help yourselves.

Now it is my great honour to introduce to you the man behind The Farkley Global Youth Plan, the man whose vision and integrity and great humanity has turned the wheels for a great event such as this. Ladies and gentlemen, please join me –

[*The Macedonian dancers burst onto the stage again and the music has to be stopped; the dancers ushered off. Meanwhile the Greek National Anthem bursts forth and the* GREEK ORTHODOX ARCHBISHOP *is spotlit as he makes his way to his seat, carrying his gold spectre. As he sits down we see him dragged backwards off stage by* PIGGY *in his terrorist outfit.* FARKLEY *steps forward into the spotlight.*]

FARKLEY: Men and women of Australia. I have a vision.

CROWD: Stop the rot!

DELIA: Free East Timor!

CROWD: Indonesia out!
What do we want?
Indonesia out!
When do we want it?
Now!!

[*This is accompanied by much stamping of feet and cheering etc.*]

FARKLEY: I have a vision.

MERLE: Stop the genocide of Black Australia!

CROWD: Murderers! Murderers!

[*There ensues a general rabble from every interest group represented. Chanting, banner waving, etc.* DAWN *grabs the microphone and fires a pistol in the air. A group of menacing SS type security men race onto the stage with pistols aimed at the* CROWD.]

DAWN: Silence! Or we'll shoot!

[*Suddenly an eerie silence descends.*]

Thank you. Now before the Honorable Member of Greater Burke will resume his visionary rhetoric, I want you all to take your seats. Sit down and shut up. Got it? We are here to talk about peace, right? Peace and harmony and if I so much as hear a peep from any one of you, there'll be blood shed. Do you understand me! Now. Kimble.

[*An SS Officer is aiming a gun directly at* FARKLEY. *He is disconcerted.*]

FARKLEY: Right. I ... um ... It is my great pleasure to introduce The Farkley Global Youth Plan to you tonight, as a means of working together, side by side, shoulder to shoulder to create a vision for the future. The architect of this grand scheme was none other than our very own Dragi Smilevski.

DRAGI [*leaning into the microphone, terrified*]: It wasn't my idea.

FARKLEY: Ah modesty, Mr Smilevski. He is in fact the man responsible and tonight I want to give Mr Smilevski the key to our city. But first as a gesture toward global peace and harmony we have with us the Archbishop of the Greek Orthodox Church, Mr Spiros Pappas.

[PIGGY *walks on stage, dressed in the garb.*]

Would our friends from the media like to gather round closer.

[DRAGI *stands up.*]

DRAGI: As a senior member of the Macedonian community, I would like to make this symbolic gesture to our friends The Greeks, in the name of peace and harmony.

[DRAGI *offers* PIGGY *a giant salami.* FARKLEY *has positioned himself smiling obsequiously in the middle.*]

PIGGY: And as the Archbishop said to the thief, I would like to make this symbolic gesture in return –

[*He slams the salami down onto* DRAGI's *head. They scuffle with all the security men leaping on top. The* CROWD *roars and it's on for young and old. Suddenly* PIGGY *grabs the microphone.*]

There's dog meat in the salami. Don't eat the salami.

[*The* CROWD *screams. People rush off to vomit. Suddenly shots are fired again and* POLICE *rush onto the stage.*]

POLICE: Hold it! Hold it right there! We are investigating the whereabouts of one Brian Guest.

DAWN: That's him! Over there!

[*They drag a cowering* BRIAN *onto centre stage.*]

POLICE: Brian Guest you are under arrest for the possession of stolen goods and harbouring a dangerous dog.

BRIAN [*to* TREV]: You told me the dog was dead!

PIGGY: It is. It's in the salami sandwiches.

POLICE: Silence! Dragi Smilevski. Which one is Dragi Smilevski?

DAWN: That's him. Over there.

POLICE: Dragi Smilevski you are under arrest for suspected meat substitution.

DRAGI: I did nothing –

POLICE: Silence!

DRAGI: No!

POLICE: Arrest him!

POLICE: And you Kimble Farkley, what are you doing?

DAWN: I think he's vomitting.

POLICE: Get over here, this minute.

[*Pause.*]

There's a phone call for you.

[*One of his junior officers hands* FARKLEY *the mobile.*]

FARKLEY: I think there must be some mistake.

POLICE: There's no mistake, buddy. It's the Premier. You've kept him waiting for two hours.

FARKLEY: Hello. Hello. There's nobody there.

[*He hands the phone to* DAWN *inadvertently.*]

POLICE: Pity about that Mr Farkley I think he wanted to tell you himself.

FARKLEY: What did he want to tell me?

POLICE: Come on. Round 'em up! Off to the Station.

FARKLEY: Excuse me. Excuse me. What did the Premier want to say?

DAWN: Hello. Hello Mr Premier. Why thank you. Thank you very much. I'll tell him myself. [*To* FARKLEY] You're fired Farkley!

[*The* CROWD *roars. Suddenly as dramatic music swells and the criminals are being dragged off,* DAWN *finds herself in the Mayoral Chair which rises and rises to the ceiling.*]

Why Mr Premier. Thank you. Lord Mayor? Well I'll have to think about that one very carefully. Of course we'd have to discuss the package. I mean two hundred thousand dollars would be very modest I'd say.

[*Suddenly we hear barking. And Kenny races onto the stage, barking excitedly at* DAWN. TREV *races onto the stage, closes his eyes and points a gun.*]

Kenny! Kenny!

[*A loud gun shot rings out. Blackout.*]

THE END

130